HELLENISTIC GREEK GRAMMAR
AND NOAM CHOMSKY

SOCIETY
OF BIBLICAL
LITERATURE

DISSERTATION SERIES

William Baird, Editor

Number 62

HELLENISTIC GREEK GRAMMAR AND
NOAM CHOMSKY:
Nominalizing Transformations

by Daryl Dean Schmidt

Daryl Dean Schmidt

HELLENISTIC
GREEK GRAMMAR
AND
NOAM CHOMSKY:
NOMINALIZING
TRANSFORMATIONS

Scholars Press

Distributed by
SCHOLARS PRESS
101 Salem St.
P.O. Box 2268
Chico, California 95927

HELLENISTIC GREEK GRAMMAR AND

NOAM CHOMSKY:

Nominalizing Transformations

Daryl Dean Schmidt

Ph.D., 1979   Department of Religion   Advisor:
Berkeley, California   Texas Christian University   Edward C
                       Ft. Worth, Texas 76129

Library of Congress Cataloging in Publication Data

Schmidt, Daryl Dean.
    Hellenistic Greek grammar and Noam Chomsky.

    (Dissertation series / Society of Biblical
Literature ; no. 62)
    Originally presented as the author's thesis
(doctoral—Graduate Theological Union)
    Bibliography: p.
    1. Greek language, Hellenistic (300 B. C.–600
A. D.)—Grammar—Study and teaching. 2. Greek
language, Hellenistic (300 B. C.—600 A. D.)—
Grammar, Generative. 3. Chomsky, Noam. I. Title.
II. Series: Dissertation series (Society of
Biblical Literature) ; no. 62.
PA607.S3 1981   487'.4   81-13544
ISBN 0-89130-527-0   AACR2

Printed in the United States of America
1 2 3 4 5
Edwards Brothers, Inc.
Ann Arbor, Michigan 48106

CONTENTS

ACKNOWLEDGEMENTS

I gratefully acknowledge the assistance received in the preparation of this dissertation for publication. I would like to thank the Office of Research and Sponsored Projects at Texas Christian University for their financial support and also my student assistant, Mark Plunkett, for the valuable time he spent typing and preparing the indices.

PREFACE

My interest in the study of New Testament Greek grammar
egan when I entered M.Div. studies at the Associated Mennonite
iblical Seminaries. Among my most enjoyable seminary classes
as the first year of required Greek taught by Gertrude Roten.
thank her for instilling in me a fondness for the Greek
anguage that grew into the basis for my doctoral dissertation.

The opportunity to nurture that growth at the Graduate
heological Union was provided by the Church Divinity School of
he Pacific, and especially by Professor Edward C. Hobbs. During
y years of course work with him and six years as Teaching Fellow
nder his supervision, he generously shared his linguistic in-
ights about the nature of language and his conviction that Noam
homsky's theory of language had profound implications for the
tudy and teaching of Greek grammar. These implications became
oncrete in the summer language school at CDSP the past four
ears, where Teaching Fellow Irene Lawrence and I worked together
ith Professor Hobbs on *An Outline of a Transformational-
enerative Grammar of Hellenistic Greek*. I am grateful to them
or that learning experience, out of which emerged the shape of
his study.

I would also like to acknowledge the research support
hich made possible my contributions to that *Outline Grammar*.
hanks to the generous gift of Mr. Thomas E. Cummins and a
atching grant from I.B.M., a Hellenistic Greek Linguistics
roject was initiated by the Center for Hermeneutical Studies
n Hellenistic and Modern Culture, under the direction of Pro-
essor Hobbs, and with Lawrence and myself as Research Fellows.
he work of that project, as reflected in the *Outline Grammar*,
s the framework within which I undertook my dissertation studies.

The dissertation itself owes much as every stage to the
enerous manner in which Professor Hobbs has offered his time
nd attention, from helping to formulate the first outline to

carefully directing its finish, all the while letting it be my own endeavor, which, needless to say, resulted in my own conclusions. Thus, I express my sincere gratitude to Edward Hobbs.

However, many other persons have also been important to this dissertation. First of all, I want to thank the other readers: Julian Boyd, University of California, Berkeley (also for his seminar on AUX), Michael Guinan, Franciscan School of Theology, and Wilhelm Wuellner, Pacific School of Religion, who were all very supportive and always asked helpful questions and made constructive suggestions.

I also want to acknowledge the help of many staff people especially Barbara Arnold and Elizabeth Over at the GTU, Billie Gendron at the GTU Library and Esther Davis at CDSP.

Finally, for the encouragement I have received since the day we first met in Greek class, and for making these last dissertation years enjoyable ones, I especially thank Babs Marie, for being a good student, a faithful friend and a loving wife.

INTRODUCTION

The study of grammar in the modern era has gone through several momentous periods, and each one has been conditioned primarily by a preceding change in linguistic theory. In each case the change has occurred rather suddenly and has had a revolutionary effect on the study of grammar. The study of Hellenistic Greek grammar has followed this same pattern, though always one revolution behind that in linguistics.

The current revolution in linguistics has significantly altered our understanding of syntax. There are only a few basic syntactic constructions (phrase structure rules) which are universal to all languages. However, each language develops its own (transformational) system for allowing one phrase structure to function syntactically in another (as an embed). This offers the first comprehensive linguistic theory for explaining the formation of complex sentences as a series of embedding transformations.

We begin our study with a look at the major Hellenistic Greek grammars that have been in use during the past century and at the linguistic framework upon which each is built. The current ones are all products of 19th century linguistics, including the one most widely used in scholarship, Debrunner's edition of Blass. A classical philologist recently addressed the question, "What happened to New Testament Greek grammar after Albert Debrunner?" and could only conclude, "Today research into post-classical Greek in general and NT Greek in particular has come almost to a standstill."[1] Contemporary linguistics can provide the stimulus for revitalizing the study of New Testament Greek grammar as it has done for many other languages.

In the second chapter we present the development in contemporary linguistics of Noam Chomsky's transformational-generative theory of grammar, from its antecedents in structuralism to its "extended standard theory" version. Our focus is particularly on that part of the syntax which covers embedding transformations.[2]

1

Transformational-generative grammar is the basis, then, for our investigation in the last chapter of one type of embedding transformation in Hellenistic Greek, namely, nominalizatio i.e., embedded sentences functioning as noun phrases. We seek to formulate the nominalizing transformations that are part of Hellenistic Greek grammar. We are primarily interested in the New Testament authors, but the transformations are those used by all Hellenistic writers (excluding clearly Atticizing or Semiticizing constructions).

Having demonstrated the effectiveness of transformationa generative grammar in explaining nominalizations in Hellenistic Greek, we will have thereby indicated the need for a new gramma of Hellenistic Greek and an important direction in which resear could continue.

How we understand the structure of human language in gen eral and how we understand the syntax of a particular language have a direct impact on all the hermeneutical questions that apply to studying texts written in that language. Since the methodologies involved in New Testament studies frequently appeal to "linguistic evidence" in support of much of their work, the linguistics of Hellenistic Greek grammar is not peripheral to the discipline of New Testament hermeneutics. The practical implications of this are indicated in the various ways we apply those methodologies in our use of New Testament references--in textual criticism, source analysis, stylistics, translation and interpretation. Concrete studies in each of those areas would benefit from an advance in our understanding of the language of the New Testament.

CHAPTER ONE

THE PRESENT STATE OF THE STUDY OF
HELLENISTIC GREEK GRAMMAR

The study of Hellenistic Greek grammar has passed through
several distinct phases in the modern era (as the Introduction
points out), and in each case the change has been occasioned by
a new linguistic development. However, the new approach usually
was first applied to Classical Greek before it influenced the
study of Hellenistic Greek (HG). Thus by the time a new "revolutionary" grammar appeared for HG, its linguistic basis had
been superseded by another revolution in linguistics, making
each such grammar anachronistic from its inception.

The major HG grammars of the last two centuries have followed in the wake of three linguistic periods: (1) rationalist,
in the first half of the 19th century, (2) comparative-historical,
in the second half of the 19th century, and (3) structuralist,
in the first half of the 20th century. Meanwhile, linguistics
has since encountered another major revolution: transformational-
generative (discussed in the next chapter). We will look briefly at these periods in the study of HG grammar.

A rationalist theory of language, which has been associated with Descartes,[1] became dominant in the 17th century. It
is best exemplified in the French Port-Royal *Grammar*.[2] It was
over a century before such a rational investigation was applied
to Greek by Gottfried Hermann,[3] and another two decades before
George B. Winer incorporated Hermann's approach into a grammar
on New Testament Greek.[4] Winer's grammar dominated the field
in the 19th century and became the first widely-used New Testament Greek grammar.[5]

Our interest in Winer's rational grammar goes beyond its
historical significance, however, since Chomsky claims that the
Port-Royal *Grammar* was essentially proto-transformational-gener-
ative.[6] In fact, the way Winer contrasted his rational approach

3

with the predominant empiricism of the preceding century seems
to anticipate Chomsky's attack on behaviorism. This is reflect
already at the beginning of Winer's preface:

> When this Grammar first appeared, in 1822, the object
> proposed was, to check the unbounded arbitrariness with
> which the language of the New Testament had so long been
> handled in Commentaries and exegetical prelections, and,
> so far as the case admitted, to apply the results of the
> rational philology, as obtained and diffused by Hermann
> and his school, to the Greek of the New Testament. It
> was in truth needful that some voice should be raised
> which might call to account the deep-rooted empiricism
> of the expositors, and might strive to rescue the New
> Testament writers from the bondage of a perverted philol-
> ogy, which, while it styled itself sacred, showed not the
> slightest respect for the sacred authors and their well-
> considered phraseology.
> The fundamental error . . . of this biblical philol-
> ogy, and consequently of the exegesis which was based
> upon it, really consisted in this, that neither the
> Hebrew language nor the Greek of the New Testament was
> regarded as a *living* idiom . . . designed for a medium
> of human intercourse. [7]

Then in his Introduction Winer explained the object of his stud

> The peculiar language of the N.T., like every other
> language, presents two distinct aspects for scientific
> investigation . . . the *material* element; . . . the *formal*
> element. The former is the province of lexicography; the
> latter of grammar,--which must be carefully distinguished
> from the laws of style (or rhetoric) of the N.T. . . . .
> As the language in which the N.T. was written is a
> variety of Greek, the proper object of a N.T. grammar
> would be fully accomplished by a systematic grammatical
> comparison of the N.T. language with the written Greek
> of the same age and of the same description.

However, no study existed of such comparable material, nor, eve
more desirable, was there "a grammar of the language used by
the Greek-speaking inhabitants of Alexandria, gathered from al
parts of the world." So Winer made the necessary adjustment:

> The boundaries of N.T. grammar must be extended in
> two directions. It must first . . . investigate the
> peculiarities of the later Greek in the N.T., . . .
> and secondly, it must point out the modifications which
> were introduced by the influence of the Hebrew-Aramean
> on the Greek . . . It is not possible, however, to make
> a rigorous distinction between these two elements; for
> in the mind of the N.T. writers the mixture of the (later)
> Greek with the national (Jewish) has given rise to a
> *single* syntax, which must be recognized and exhibited in
> its unity. [8]

Winer then described the method he sought to apply:

The *rational* method of treatment, which seeks for
the explanation of all the phenomena of languages, even
of their anomalies, in the modes of thought which char-
acterise nations and individual writers, has completely
transformed [*hat . . . ganz umgestaltet*: "has accomplished a complete revolution" in Masson and Thayer]
the study of Greek. The same method must be applied to
the language of the N.T. . . .
It was in Greek philology that the reformation com-
menced. A pupil of Reitz, Gottfr. Hermann, by his work
De emendanda ratione grammaticae Graecae (1801) gave
the first powerful impulse to the *rational* [*philoso-
phisch* in previous German editions, both here and above]
investigation of this noble language. . . . The principles of this method, which entitle it to the name of
rational, are the following:
(a) The fundamental meaning of every grammatical
form (case, tense, mood), or the idea which underlay
this form in the mind of the Greek nation, is exactly
seized, and all the various uses of the form are de-
duced from this primary signification. . .
(b) When the established laws of the language are
violated, either in expressions of general currency,
or in the usage of individual writers, the grammarian
is at pains to show how the irregularity originated
in the mind of the speaker or writer, . . .
The language is thus presented as bearing the direct
impress of Greek thought, and appears as a *living* idiom.[9]

Winer gave this last point some considerable emphasis.

He was very clear that Hellenistic Greek was

a language of common life, a popular spoken language,
in which the peculiarities of the various dialects . . .
were fused together. . . . This spoken Greek . . .
is the true basis of the language of the LXX and the
Apocrypha, and also of the N.T. language. . . .
The Jews of Egypt and Syria . . . learned Greek in
the first instance by intercourse with those who spoke
Greek, not from books; hence we need not wonder that
in writing they usually retained the peculiarities of
the popular spoken language.[10]

The argument for New Testament Greek as a living spoken
language received its strongest support with the newly discovered
secular papyri at the end of Winer's century. However, even
though Deissmann[11] claimed that the papyri established the exis-
tence of a Hellenistic vernacular language which was used by the
New Testament writers, Winer was not confirmed in his insights
about the nature of New Testament Greek, because the grammarians
who appropriated Deissmann's results were working with the new
comparative philology and its historical perspective. So they
rejected the rational, anti-empiricist position of Winer and
consequently overlooked any contributions he might have made.

The rise of comparative philology had rendered rational grammar
obsolete.

Comparative philology actually began before the publication of Winer's first grammar in 1822, with the work of Franz
Bopp on a comparative study of classical Indo-European languages.[12] This began a century-long emphasis in classical language study on the growth and develpment of related languages
and dialects by comparing their analogous forms. By the end of
the 19th century the results of comparative-historical philology
began to be applied to the study of HG grammar, in Germany,
England and America. Each of the three endeavors emerged as a
major tradition, yielding one of the standard reference works
on the subject still in use today: Blass-Debrunner, Moulton-
Howard-Turner and Robertson.

The first of these was begun in Germany, in 1896, by
Friedrich Blass,[13] a classical philologist (not a comparative
philologist). He was primarily concerned to investigate "the
special features" of New Testament Greek, which could not be
thoroughly documented in "the general grammar of the Greek language."[14] A working knowledge of Greek grammar was thus presupposed[15] as the framework within which to catalogue the chang
in the Greek language between the classical and New Testament
eras. These observations on changes have mostly to do with for
and usage, the matters of direct interest to the philologist of
that day.[16]

After his death the initial work of Blass was carried on
by Albert Debrunner, who was not only a classical philologist,
but also an Indo-European linguist. He revised and expanded th
material through several new editions from 1913 till 1958, afte
which Robert Funk produced an English translation.[17] Though
Debrunner added his own contributions from comparative philology, he reaffirmed the approach of Blass: "the major emphasis
in the treatment of NT syntax must fall, where Blass had demonstrated his mastery, namely, on the comparision of NT with clas
sical syntax."[18] This emphasis kept the Blass-Debrunner gramma
clearly in the tradition of classical philology, by treating
New Testament Greek rather like a dialect, or one historical
period in the history of the Greek language. Within that frame
work Debrunner also extended the comparisons to include the

newly discovered papyri, and early Christian literature, but he did not want to expand it into a "Hellenistic grammar."

The tradition of Blass and Debrunner has been rigorously preserved in a recent new edition,[19] eighty years after Blass began, which still reflects nothing of the linguistic developments of the 20th century.

The combination of classics and comparative philology brought about interestingly different results in the background of James Hope Moulton, the British scholar who initiated *A Grammar of New Testament Greek* as a three-volume project at the turn of the century. His impetus came from his father, William F. Moulton, who had translated several editions of Winer's *Grammar* and had intended to write a new edition of it himself before he died. When his son undertook the task, he explicitly said on the title page of the first edition, that it was "based on W. F. Moulton's edition of G. B. Winer's Grammar." The second edition, that same year, moved the expression of indebtedness to Winer from the title page to the Preface.

Moulton lived to complete only half of the project himself.[20] Wilbert F. Howard edited and finished the work on the second volume.[21] The volume on syntax was delayed by several deaths before Nigel Turner finally "broke the spell by living to complete Volume III" several decades later.[22] He recently added another volume on style,[23] which does little more than reorganize the earlier material according to the various New Testament writers. At that time the earlier volumes were again reprinted. So the four-volume grammar covers the first three-quarters of this century, long enough to notice a shift in the linguistic understanding of New Testament Greek.

Moulton's preface set the tone for his approach to this grammar:

> The life-history of the Greek language has been investigated with minutest care, not only in the age of its glory, but also throughout the centuries of its supposed senility and decay. Its syntax has been illumined by the comparative method; and scholars have arisen who have been willing to desert the masterpieces of literature [as Moulton did himself!] and trace the humble development of the Hellenistic vernacular down to its lineal descendant in the vulgar tongue of the present day. . . . The main purpose of these *Prolegomena* has been to provide a sketch of the language of the New

> Testament as it appears to those who have followed Deiss-
> mann into a new field of research. . . . In the second
> volume I shall try to present as concisely as I can the
> systematic facts of Hellenistic accidence and syntax,
> not in the form of an appendix to a grammar of clas-
> sical Greek, but giving the later language the inde-
> pendent dignity which it deserves.[24]

In the opening of his first chapter he then talked about
his new understanding of New Testament Greek. He himself had
earlier called it *Hebraic* Greek, *colloquial* Greek, and *late* Greek
before substituting the label *common* Greek, and then *Hellenistic*

> The disappearance of that word "Hebraic" from its prom-
> inent place in our delineation of NT language marks a
> change in our conceptions of the subject nothing less
> than revolutionary. This is not a revolution in theory
> alone. It touches exegesis at innumerable points. It
> demands large modifications in our very latest gram-
> mars . . . .[25]

Deissmann's work on the papyri had demonstrated to Moulton
"that 'Biblical' Greek, except when it is translation Greek,
was simply the vernacular of daily life."[26]

> What we can assert with assurance is that the papyri
> have finally destroyed the figment of a NT Greek
> which in any material respect differed from that spo-
> ken by ordinary people in daily life throughout the
> Roman world.[27]

Moulton was able to make this assertion even more emphat-
ically than Winer had earlier, because of his "Deissmannian"
vantage point in applying comparative philology to Greek. However, the comparative methodology had no unifying theory about
the nature of language. So even at its best, Moulton's understanding could only produce a more complete catalogue and description of forms and usage for HG. Unfortunately, Moulton's
project had to be completed by others, at a time when "Deissmannism" was under attack for failing to see the influential
role of Semitisms in HG. Moulton's pupil, Howard, in editing
Vol. II, wrote the Appendix on "Semitisms in the New Testament"
which Moulton had intended to write. Howard favorably cited
the work of Deissmann's critics and claimed that Moulton himself
was moving in that direction.[28] Already Moulton's legacy was
becoming tarnished.

By the time Turner wrote the volume on syntax, some thirt
years later, "Deissmannism" had waned considerably, and Turner
promoted its overthrow, thereby devaluing Moulton's understandin

of the subject matter. One of Turner's concerns was "the relationship of Biblical Greek to classical and Hellenistic."[29]
The language of the New Testament was for him "Biblical Greek,"
an entity distinct from "Hellenistic Greek." The implications
of that view are clear in his Introduction:

> I have tried to expose consistently the almost com-
> plete absence of classical standards in nearly every
> author. . . . It is not that Biblical Greek has no
> standards at all, but pains must be taken to discover
> them outside the sphere of classical Greek, even out-
> side secular Greek altogether, although the living
> Koine must be kept in mind always. . . .
>   . . . the present work does suggest that Bibl.
> Greek is a unique language with a unity and charac-
> ter of its own. . . . There is a family likeness
> among these Biblical works, setting them apart from
> the papyri and from contemporary literary Greek, al-
> though the books from Semitic sources may have these
> features to an especial degree. . . .
>   . . . the lapse of half a century was needed to
> assess the discoveries of Deissmann and Moulton and
> put them in their right perspective. We now have to
> conclude that not only is the subject-matter of the
> Scriptures unique but so also is the language in
> which they have come to be written or translated.[30]

A definite linguistic regression is evidenced here.
Turner is so taken in by New Testament peculiarities and Semitisms (the largest section in his index) that he is no longer
even certain "whether it was a spoken language."[31] Later, when
he wrote Vol. IV, he was describing the "inner homogeneity of
Biblical Greek" as the "layer of basic Jewish Greek" which can
be found in all New Testament authors.[32]

Thus the grammar which bears Moulton's name ends up by
denying his "central position, that the New Testament was written in the normal κοινή of the Empire."[33] And thus comparative
philology had succeeded in erasing its last significant link to
Winer, having long before put aside his rational approach to
grammar. The revolution introduced by Winer had been overthrown
by another revolution, but not that envisioned by Moulton. He
used "revolutionary"[34] for the understanding of Hellenistic
Greek as a living spoken language. But when the publication
announcement said of the Moulton grammar, "a revolution in New
Testament study,"[35] it referred more to the comparative method
being applied to New Testament Greek than it did to Moulton's
"revolutionary" understanding of the New Testament Greek language.

In America the results of comparative philology were care
fully applied to New Testament Greek by A. T. Robertson.[36] He
too had begun with the notion of a revised edition of Winer (before Moulton's project was announced), but "so much progress
had been made in comparative philology and historical grammar
since Winer wrote his great book that it seemed senseless to go
on with it."[37] Comparative philology had wrought a "linguistic
revolution" that for Robertson was integrally linked to historical grammar.[38] The historical-comparative method had yielded
extensive results on classical Greek[39] and now had to be applied
to the vernacular Greek of the New Testament, an historical phas
of the Greek language made distinct by the work of Deissmann.
With such an emphasis on the comparative history of language,
which Robertson developed as a scholarly heir of Bopp,[40] he
aimed for a "descriptive historical grammar"[41] that would recor
the grammatical usage of a particular time (the New Testament
era), and compare that to some earlier standard (Attic), and to
other particular times and places (LXX, papyri, and literary
Koine). Robertson thus produced a massive volume of observatio
about the various changes the Greek language had undergone, and
an extensive catalogue of usages in the New Testament, but historical and comparative grammar lacked the facility to go beyon
such a description of how a language was used. However, Robertson made a virtue of that limitation. The scientific linguist
appealed "to the actual facts of the history of language," rath
than to logic.[42] It was clear to Robertson how far linguistics
had come:

> It is a long step from Winer, three generations ago, to
> the present time. We shall never go back again to that
> standpoint. Winer was himself a great emancipator in
> the grammatical field. But the battles that he fought
> are now ancient history.[43]

As Robertson was making that definitive statement, the next rev
olution in linguistics was already underway. It set the tone
for the 20th century.

The new approach came to be called "structuralism." Its
origins are traced to Ferdinand de Saussure, the Swiss linguist
From 1906 till 1911 he taught three courses on general linguistics. After his death, his students compiled their class notes
into the only preserved account of de Sausssure's method.[44]

De Saussure directly attacked comparative philology by emphasizing four major distinctions which contrasted it with his
approach. On the one hand, comparative philology dealt with
written texts, as the user's *"parole"* (actual speech), from a
diachronic perspective tracing historical developments, with the
focus on the *substance* of language's realizations. De Saussure
sought rather for linguistics to study the living *spoken* language,
in terms of the user's *"langue"* (the language a speaker knows),
from a *synchronic* perspective analyzing the complete language
at a given time, with the focus on the *form* of language's
structure, as discovered in the relational patterns of the
whole language.[45]

Structuralism became the dominant feature of 20th century
American linguistics. Especially prominant was Leonard Bloomfield[46] in the 1930's, whose work became the definitive influence
on all later descriptive linguistics. He rejected mentalistic
notions of language for a behaviorist view which promoted
empirical observation of linguistic units, first phonological,
then morphological, finally whole words, and then groups of
words. The process used to find these units is called immediate
constituent (IC) analysis. Each unit is broken down to its
smaller units, until eventually the basic elements are discovered,
which can then be appropriately classified. The strengths of
this system are best seen in the productive investigation which
was made of American Indian languages during the early decades
of the 20th century.[47] By mid-century, the neo-Bloomfieldians
began synthesizing their results. The best known among this
school was Noam Chomsky's teacher, Zellig Harris, who will be
discussed in Chapter Two in connection with a fuller treatment
of structural linguistics.

In the 1950's the results of structuralism were applied
to the study and teaching of English grammar. Previously structuralism had been most concerned with the smallest linguistic
units, how phonemes and morphemes make up words,[48] and only
secondarily with an "immediate constituent" analysis of full
sentences. By the early 1950's, however, syntax had become of
increasing interest. In the study of English grammar, that
concern was most successfully exemplified by Charles C. Fries.[49]
His approach was popularized for the teaching of English by

Paul Roberts.[50]   Subsequent work on the teaching of English by
Roberts[51] and on the systematic study of English by H. A. Gleason[52] kept abreast of the newest developments in linguistics,
namely, the initial stages of transformational-generative (TG)
grammar.

Structuralism began to be applied to the study of New
Testament Greek without the usual benefit of an earlier thorough
application to classical Greek.   It was also the more limited
pre-TG structuralism.   The most serious such effort is by Robert
Funk.[53]   Realizing "that a revolution had taken place in the
study and learning of language,"[54] he saw an opportunity finally
to overcome to ineffectiveness of traditional grammar in teachir
Greek.   He uses the descriptive linguistic framework as presente
in Gleason, reinforced by the structuralism of Roberts.   Funk
explains his method thus:

> In accordance with the aims of descriptive analy-
> sis, it was determined to proceed empirically insofar
> as possible [i.e., with the analysis of a selected cor-
> pus of texts].[55]

> A descriptive grammar must achieve two things:
> 1) it must develop a classification of words and other
> elements; 2) it must state the grammatical relations
> that obtain among these elements. . . .
> The classification of words and other elements must
> be based on structural, i.e., grammatical, features. . . .
> If classification is derived from structure, there are
> two sets of criteria which may be used, and these do
> not always coincide: 1) One set of criteria may be de-
> rived from the words themselves, i.e., from morpholog-
> ical criteria; 2) Another set may be derived from the
> ways a word may be used in a sentence. . . .
> . . . an extensive statement of the relations be-
> tween these features proves to be a very complicated
> matter.   It is made no less complicated by the fact
> that various word classes require subdivision into
> smaller classes, and many words belong to more than
> one class.[56]

Here we have a typical structuralist design, which Funk finds
very fitting for a highly inflected language such as Greek.   He
devotes his major effort to Greek morphology, labeling and classifying all the structural signals (prefixes and suffixes) and
function words (negatives, interrogatives, subordinators).   Thi
process is sometimes called taxonomy, or even "verbal botany."[5]

Funk's presentation on syntax is likewise an attempt to
list all the common sentence patterns, again a notion taken fror

Gleason, who uses Robert's schema. Gleason, however, went on to
adopt the results of early generative and then transformational
grammars to show, e.g., the integral relationship between an active sentence and its passive counterpart; a question, and the
statement corresponding to it. In contrast, Funk only uses the
label "transformation" in various places for the passive, but
his failure to comprehend its significance is reflected in the
fact that the passive sentences are dispersed under the various
appropriate categories of their sentence structure, and other
corresponding types of sentences are not dealt with at all. In
the final analysis, Funk's effort is an excellent witness both
to the shortcomings of structuralism: elaborate classification
of items without an adequate description of syntax, and to its
major contribution: morphological analysis of word forms and
types. The syntactical inadequacy of structuralism was addressed
head-on by the new revolution in linguisitics. Chomsky's transformational-generative theory had even undergone its most significant revision before Funk's grammar was written. Once again
a new Hellenistic Greek grammar was making its appearance just
when its linguistic basis was losing currency.

     This brief survey has shown that the study of Hellenistic
Greek grammar has consistently been based on a linguistic theory
that had already been supplanted by the next major development
in linguistics. We are again in that same situation. A new
revolution in linguistics has completely altered the way language is conceptualized, studied and taught, both theoretically
and pedagogically (for everything from ancient Egyptian to elementary school English). After a closer look at this theory we
will apply it to one aspect of Hellenistic Greek.

CHAPTER TWO

CONTEMPORARY LINGUISTIC THEORY

The latest, and perhaps most pervasive, revolution in linguistics has been the one sparked by Noam Chomsky,[1] dating from the publication in 1957 of *Syntactic Structures*.[2] Here was not just a new or improved methodology, but a complete redefinition of the agenda of linguistics.[3] In order to grasp the full dimensions of this revolution, we need first to summarize the forefront of pre-Chomskyan linguistics.

Chomsky was a graduate student of Zellig Harris at the University of Pennsylvania.[4] Harris represents the culmination of neo-Bloomfieldian descriptive linguistics. In fact, what follows is characteristic of the work done by all structural linguists from Bloomfield on, often called simply "structuralism." Harris' *Methods in Structural Linguistics* is a program of "research methods . . . arranged in the form of the successive procedures of analysis imposed by the working linguist upon his data,"[5] which is a recorded corpus of utterances. The process begins by identifying the smallest distinct units of language, the phoneme (similar segments of sound), and then investigating the "distribution or arrangement" of individual segments in relation to others. Classifications are set up next based on the patterns of which segments regularly occur in the same context with others.

The entire process is then repeated for morphemes, each morpheme being a group of phonemes that occurs in a fixed combination or in a restricted distribution ("environment") of an utterance. Thus one-syllable words are morphemes, as are some multisyllable words like "ceiling" (because "ceil" does not occur in any other environment), but "sailing" is two morphemes ("sail" and "-ing" occur, respectively, as a fixed form, and in a similar restricted environment, i.e., a verbal suffix). By segmenting utterances into morphemes, the morphemes can be classified

15

by substitutability (e.g., "small" and "large" are the same
class because they are both acceptable in the sequence "The
_____ ball"). The sequences of morphemes become the constructions which are grouped into "syntactic form-classes which indicate what morpheme sequences have identical syntactic function
i.e., occur in identical environments in the utterance." So
syntax is really a subdivision of morphology, in that the linguist first identifies the syntactic function of morphemes and
then "builds up from them to even larger morpheme sequences having identical syntactic status."[6]

The impression is left at this stage of an efficiently organized set of procedures which begins with the smallest units
and methodically works its way from the ground up, constructing
ever more interrelated sequences until it reaches the complete
utterance, and all this with the linguist functioning very me-
chanically as a "true scientist." However, it is at the top
level, the utterance, that the analysis requires more than mere
labeling and classifying of forms. An excerpt from the problem
as presented by Harris:

> We take, for example, the utterance *She made him a good
> husband because she made him a good wife*. We know that
> there is a difference in meaning between the two occur-
> rences of *made*; and since we know this without any out-
> side information beyond hearing the sentence, it follows
> that indication of the *difference in meaning* [emphasis
> added] and in construction can be derived from the struc-
> ture of the utterance. The difference is not in the mor-
> pheme *made*, since the two occurrences are identical in
> form, and must therefore be in the class membership of
> *made* in the two cases. But the class membership must be
> recognizable from the different class sequences and their
> substitution in the two utterances. (The second can be
> paraphrased, She made a good wife *for him*; the first can-
> not use such a paraphrase.)[7]

The linguist has to recognize "difference in meaning" between
two identical sequences in order to be able to classify them
separately. No amount of precise sub-categorizing at the level
of individual units is going to remove or reduce the problem.
The linguist is not an indifferent operator of a precision in-
strument after all. Harris (like all users of language) was in-
formed by his own intuitive knowledge of the language that these
two occurrences of *made* had to be classified differently.

When this process has been successfully completed for a large
enough corpus, the language will be thoroughly labeled and

classified and then one can take any new utterance, reverse the
process and begin at the top by determining the immediate constituents of the utterance, and the immediate constituents of each
one of those constituents, and so on down the line until arriving
at the individual morphemes. Using Harris' notations (whose sub-
divisions are of no interest to us here), we can summarize the
reverse process for one of his utterances:[8]

$$\text{utterance} = N^4 \text{ (noun phrase) and } V^4 \text{ (verb phrase)}$$
$$= T \text{ and } N^3; \ V^2 \text{ and } Vv$$
$$= T, \ N^2, \text{ and } -s; \ Vv, \ V^1 \text{ and } P$$
$$= T, \ A \text{ and } N^2, \ -s; \ Vv, \ V^1 \text{ and } P$$
$$= T, \ D, \ A \text{ and } N^2, \ -s; \ Vv, \ V^1 \text{ and } P.$$

Doing this to a variety of different types of utterances allows
for generalizing about the relations of various position clauses,
i.e., larger groups of morpheme sequences which "substitute freely for each other in those positions in the utterance within
which that class occurs."[9] Harris then concludes with a brief
discussion of morphological structure, i.e., "sentence types,"
based on such generalizations. For English they are variations
of N V or N V N.

Taking from Harris' survey, we may summarize the methods
of structural linguistics. "The basic operations are those of
segmentation and classification," distinctions derived from comparision. "As a result of these operations, we not only obtain
initial elements, but are also able to define new sets of elements as classes or combinations of old ones." This is achieved
by applying "various techniques of discovery . . . used over and
over and over again . . . to find regularities and parallel or
intersecting patterns." Finally, larger and larger classes are
established through "the generalization of operations." By focussing on "considerations of discovery" we avoid "any classification of forms on the basis of meaning" (although we noted a
problem with this above). Assuming our corpus was adequately
large (a "statistical problem"), we take the results to be indicative of the structure of the whole language. The results may
even relate to other areas, such as language learning and other
sciences.[10] Below we will see how completely Chomsky upset this
procedural order.[11]

There are some later developments by Harris which also
play a role in Chomsky's work. Harris pursued his sentence-
pattern summary, with which he concluded *Methods*, by analyzing
how different sentence types are related to each other.[12] Again
the focus is on method--procedures and techniques which isolate
the distribution of various patterns and their correlation (again
using environments and classes). The method is still claimed to
be "formal, depending only on the occurrence of morphemes as
distinguishable elements," therefore not based on the meaning
of sentences. The analysis of the pattern of interrelationships
between sentences within a given text can provide information
about a language "that goes beyond descriptive linguistics"[13]
(thereby admitting that descriptive linguistics is inadequate to
fully describe the structure of a language). Harris is able to
derive twelve "grammatical transformations," using the following
definition:

Let us say that any sentence X_1 A X_2 can be "transformed"
into A *is* X_1 : A X_2.[14]

Harris' example was similar to : *The defeated team left early*
becomes *The team is defeated; the team left early*. His apparent
explanation is that *defeated* is in the same relationship to *team*
in both sentences, a relationship he calls "equivalence class."
The most common example of a transformation is the passive:

N_1 V N_2 is equivalent to N_2 *is* V-*en by* N_1 because for
any sentence like *Casals plays the cello* we can find a
sentence *The cello is played by Casals*.[15]

Harris emphasizes that meaning cannot be a factor; all
distinctions are based on morpheme patterns. He claims to keep
You wrote Paul and *Paul wrote you* from being a transformation
because of morphemic order,[16] but the passive involves the same
change of order, plus the insertion of several new morphemes.

Harris returned to this problem when he later expanded
his analysis on transformations.[17] He gave increased attention
both to the methods for "discovering transformations" and to a
much more thorough description of various transformations and of
how to identify the equivalent constructions which qualify as
transformations. His new solution to the problem noted above is
to make room for meaning:

> Transforms seem to hold invariant what might be inter-
> preted as the information content. This semantic re-
> lation is not merely because the same morphemes are
> involved. For example, *The man bit the dog* . . .
> contains the same morphemes as *The dog bit the man*
> . . ., but it describes quite a different situation;
> and [the first] is not a transform of [the second].[18]

Though in his conclusions he still tries to keep meaning outside
of linguistic structure and of transformational theory, he does
label it as an area in need of investigation.

There is one further matter raised by Harris to note here
which will concern us later. His emphasis on co-occurrence,
i.e., on finding equivalent constructions based on similar syntactic environment, leads him to treat nominals as derived from
cognate verbs. Hence, "*flight* can be identified as *fly* plus a
vn suffix and also as *flee* plus a *vn* suffix."[19] This approach
to cognates was one of the many dimensions of Harris' work which
Chomsky initially left unquestioned and only later investigated
and rejected. They will be discussed here in due course.

In summary, structuralism began with a corpus of utterances recorded from native speakers. A system of discovery procedures telling the linguist how to approach his data was then
applied to this corpus, with the goal being a precise classification of the elements of the utterances, both individually and
in their interrelationships, focussing first on phonology and
then on morphology.

We can now turn to view the nature of Chomsky's revolution. As indicated in the title *Syntactic Structures*, Chomsky
begins with syntax, a concern reached in structuralism only after
it had thoroughly researched phonology and morphology.[20] It
was necessary to reverse the point at which to begin, because
Chomsky did nothing less than challenge the objective of linguistic theory. He states his agenda clearly at the opening of
Structures:

> Syntax is the study of the principles and processes by
> which sentences are constructed in particular languages.
> Syntactic investigation of a given language has as its
> goal the construction of a grammar that can be viewed as
> a device of some sort for producing the sentences of the
> language under analysis. More generally, linguists must
> be concerned with the problem of determining the funda-
> mental underlying properties of successful grammars.
> The ultimate outcome of these investigations should be
> a theory of linguistic structure in which the descriptive

devices utilized in particular grammars are presented
and studied abstractly, with no specific reference to
particular languages. One function of this theory is
to provide a general method for selecting a grammar for
each language, given a corpus of sentences of this language.[21]

The first contrast with structuralism to note is the goa
"the construction of a grammar . . . for producing the sentence
of the language" as opposed to labeling and classifying items
in an utterance. Such a grammar will specify the rules needed
to produce or "generate" all and only the grammatical sequences
and will assign to each "a certain structural description that
specifies the linguistic elements of which it is constituted an
their structural relations (or, in the case of ambiguity, sever
such structural descriptions),"[22] while at the same time generating none of the ungrammatical sequences. The grammatical sequences are defined as those which are "acceptable to a native
speaker."[23]

From this we see the second contrast, the scope. *All*
the sentences that the grammar must generate will be infinite
in number. Therefore no one chosen corpus is adequate. The
"corpus of sentences" referred to above includes the complete
corpus that the grammar will generate, which has already been
defined to be what is acceptable to the native speaker. This
amounts to his intuitive or "implicit knowledge" of the languag
or more commonly called *competence*, in contrast to any select
corpus as the *performance* of a native speaker, i.e., how he actually uses his knowledge.

The third contrast is that of the methods developed.
Structuralism's methods were the *discovery* procedures used to
segment and classify individual elements, or in general to construct a grammar. However, no scientific discipline is concern
with how its theories are discovered, but only with their adequacy. Thus for Chomsky, the only legitimate methodological re
quirement of a linguistic theory (or any scientific theory) is
an *evaluation* procedure, which he calls a "simplicity measure."
When applied to linguistics this involves "the problem of jus-
tification of grammars"--how to choose one grammar over others
for the same language.[25]

The evaluation procedure which justifies a grammar belon
to the highest of the three levels of adequacy which are availab

to describe the success of a grammatical description for any particular linguistic theory. Chomsky succinctly summarizes his argument of this matter thus:

> The lowest level of success is achieved if the grammar presents the observed primary data correctly. A second and higher level of success is achieved when the grammar gives a correct account of the linguistic intuition of the native speaker, and specifies the observed data (in particular) in terms of significant generalizations that express underlying regularities in the language. A third and still higher level of success is achieved when the associated linguistic theory provides a general basis for selecting a grammar that achieves the second level of success over other grammars consistent with the relevant observed data that do not achieve this level of success. In this case, we can say that the linguistic theory in question suggests an explanation for the linguistic intuition of the native speaker
> . . . .
>
> For later reference, let us refer to these roughly delimited levels of success as the levels of *observational adequacy*, *descriptive adequacy*, and *explanatory adequacy*, respectively. . . . A grammar that aims for observational adequacy is concerned merely to give an account of the primary data (e.g., the corpus). . . ; a grammar that aims for descriptive adequacy is concerned to give a correct account of the linguistic intuition of the native speaker . . . ; and a linguistic theory that aims for explanatory adequacy is concerned with the internal structure of [that linguistic intuition]; that is, it aims to provide a principled basis, independent of any particular language, for the selection of the descriptively adequate grammar of each language. . . .
>
> Modern linguistics has been largely concerned with observational adequacy. In particular, this is true of post-Bloomfieldian American linguistics. . . .
>
> Traditional grammar, on the other hand, was explicitly concerned with the level of descriptive adequacy. . . .
>
> It is clear that the question of explanatory adequacy can be seriously raised only when we are presented with an explicit theory of generative grammar that specifies the form of grammars and suggests a mechanism for selecting among them (i.e., an evaluation procedure for grammars of a specified form).[26]

Observational adequacy is certainly too meager an achievement to strive for. The least we expect from a grammar is descriptive adequacy. The traditional, i.e., rational and generalizing, grammars were going in the right direction, but depended too heavily on the implicit knowledge of the reader. That is

overcome when we make explicit all the rules which are necessary
to produce, or "generate," all the acceptable sentences of a
language. Finally, we can even specify the nature of these
rules. This third level is part of general linguistic theory.
The theory prescribes the characteristics of universal generalizations about natural languages, labeled "linguistic universals."
An evaluation procedure, or "simplicity measure," is a hypothesi
about these "universal properties of language."[27]

Linguistic universals comprise one of several areas of
theoretical linguistics which have not yet been investigated in
detail. Since they fall beyond the scope of our present study,
their description must be brief.[28] They are usually classified
as *substantive* and *formal*. Substantive universals are those
items that all natural languages have in common, possibly a fixe
number of phonetic features, or limited word classes (noun, verb
adjective, etc.). Formal universals concern the rules which the
grammar contains, e.g., that a grammar must have transformationa
rules, that rules must be formulated according to specified patterns and that a grammar must indicate the order in which certai
rules apply. An evaluation procedure will then choose that gram
mar which utilizes such universals to achieve the highest degree
of descriptive adequacy.

A fundamental reason Chomsky so stressed this dimension
of linguistic theory was not that the resulting grammar would
be theoretically complete, or even aesthetically pleasing, but
that it provides a basis for a theory of mind.[29] For he asserts
that a child has "tacit knowledge of these universals."[30] They
are the major, if not the entire, part of the innate linguistic
structure which characterizes the human mind. Thus a young chil
quickly develops full creative use of its native tongue--creativ
in the precise sense of producing and comprehending sentences
never before generated in that language. The innate schema of
universals and the grammatical rules for any particular natural
language together form the grammar for that language and can be
thought of as a "language acquisition device," a model for language learning.[31] The notion of linguistic models has played ar
important role in contemporary linguistic discussion. Again we
can only consider the matter briefly.

We began our discussion of Chomsky with his description

of a grammar as a "device of some sort for producing the sen-
ences of the language under analysis." This device can also
be viewed as the "language acquisition device" which is presented
as the explanation of how a child acquires its native language.
The notion of a device for producing sentences, a generating device, is used in the sense of "an *abstract* description of how
the device functions,"[32] not the actual *hardware* which would
constitute a physically constructed implementation of it.

Chomsky formalized the notion of generative device into
a discussion of linguistic models,[33] as an outgrowth of his in-
sistence that linguistic theory must construct "general, explicit, and formal grammars."[34] He then suggested what the formalized models would look like for the grammars of the alternative
linguistic theories. The options are ordered according to increasing complexity of computer theory,[35] reflecting the fact
that this work was done during the late 1950's and early 1960's
when the federal government was funding research into machine
translation,[36] and so the description of the linguistic models
is influenced by digital computer theory.

A linguistic model, like the grammar that it represents,
must use a finite set of rules ("operations") to produce an infinite set of sentences ("output"). The simplest device meeting
that criterion is a finite-state grammar (mathematically, a "Mar-
kov process"). Such a device has a finite number of "states,"
each of which contains a set of instructions to be performed.
A very limited grammar might begin--state #1: choose (optionally
or obligatorily) one of the following words and then move to
state #2. The first state of this grammar would include the de-
terminers (articles); the second state, adjectives; the third,
nouns; the fourth, verbs; etc. A finite number of states could
produce an infinite number of sentences only by allowing for recursive operations, that is, the operations at any given state
can be repreated (e.g., more than one adjective can be chosen at
state #2). Since each state affects the choice that can be made
at the next state (matters of government and concord), this model
represents the way some linguists conceived of the process of
producing sentences in a word-ordered language like English.[37]

Chomsky has argued, however, that English is not a finite-
state language,[38] because a finite-state grammar will not

generate *all* and *only* the grammatical sentences of English. Th
principle inadequacy of a finite-state grammar is that it canno
account for self-embedding:

> Self-embedding is the fundamental property that takes a
> system outside of the generative capacity of a finite
> device, and self-embedding will ultimately result from
> nesting of dependencies.[39]

> Such elementary formal properties of natural languages
> as recursive nesting of dependencies make it impossible
> for them to be generated by finite [-state devices].[40]

Several important concepts are introduced here which need expla
nation. A "nested dependency" is, in traditional terms, a dependent clause located, or "nested," within an independent
clause. Thus in the sentence

(1) That it is raining is obvious,

"that it is raining" is nested in the sentence "(it) is obvious." Because it is located at the beginning of the sentence,
this construction is called "left-linear" nesting. English can
also produce this same sentence (to give only a simplistic explanation) by "right-linear" nesting:

(2) It is obvious that it is raining.

Nesting constructions such as these are called "embeds."

   Self-embedding is a process whereby a dependency is nest
within a sentence (neither left-linear nor right-linear), such a

(3) The man who is speaking is leaving,

where "who (i.e., the man) is speaking" is self-embedded in "th
man is leaving." Recursive nesting is embedding within another
nested dependency, as in

(4) The man who said that it is raining is leaving.

(5) The men who said that it is obvious that it is raining are
leaving.

Both of these are examples of recursive self-embedding (recursive right-embedding occurs in "I know that you know that I kno
that. . ."). A finite-state grammar cannot generate recursive
self-embedding because its individual states are linked sequen-
tially, and in self-embedding the related units are separated
arbitrarily, i.e., in (4) and (5) "the man/men" is related to
"is/are leaving," in that both parts must be either singular or
plural, regardless of the nature of the embed which is nested
between them.

To keep the two states of the noun and the verb in sequence, the embeds would have to be generated by a "grammatical
detour," optionally chosen between two of the states that generate the independent clause. Such a detour would have to contain
a complete set of states and each embed would involve its own
detour and another set of states. This would mean repeating all
the same states that generate the independent clause as many
times as there are embeds. Since there can be no theoretical
limit to the amount of self-embedding, the detours would continue
ad infinitum, each containing a complete set of states, which
then become infinite in number. Thus the requirement would be
nullified that a grammar uses *finite* means to generate an infinite number of sentences,[41] and we would no longer have a *finite*-
state grammar.

The simplest model that will generate self-embedding is
a phrase-structure (PS) model. This is in effect a formalization of immediate constituent (IC) grammar, in that it makes explicit the sort of grammar presupposed by IC analysis.[42] PS
grammar contains "rewrite rules," each of the type x——>y, interpreted as the instruction, "rewrite x as y, where x is a
single symbol and y is one or more symbols." An elementary sample of English grammar can be defined by the following rules.[43]

(6)   (a)   S ——>NP + VP

      (b)   NP ——> T + N

      (c)   VP ——> V + NP

      (d)   T ——> the

      (e)   N ——> boy, girl

      (f)   V ——> likes

From these rules we can derive the following "terminal" strings,
i.e., strings generated from the application of all the PS rules.

(7) The + boy + likes + the + girl

(8) The + girl + likes + the + boy

The application of these rules also assigns a structure to each
string--such as (9) for (7).[44]

(9)

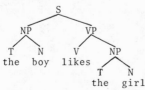

This diagram is called the "phrase marker" for this string, als
popularly known as a "tree diagram."

An actual PS grammar for English would have to be much
more complicated; e.g., it would need to account for concord of
number between nouns and verbs in every sentence, and for the
many other types of sentences in English (question, command,
condition, etc.). Theoretically, it might be possible to construct a PS grammar of English that would generate all and only
the sentences of English, i.e., a grammar that would be observa
tionally adequate for English, which a finite-state grammar is
not.

However, we have already established a higher criterion
for any grammar, viz., it must be descriptively adequate. Zell
Harris was already aware that so-called "descriptive linguistic
was inadequate to describe the relationships of sentences.[45]
Chomsky presented a more systematic critique.[46] His discussion
can be summarized under two types of common phenomena in Englis
that are not accounted for by a PS grammar: the interrelation-
ship of sentences and ambiguous sentences. Regarding the first
the native speaker of English intuitively discerns an inherent
connection between (10a) and (10b) and among the sentences
grouped within (11).

(10)   (a) The children ate the candy
       (b) The candy was eaten by the children
(11)   (a) John lives here
       (b) Who lives here?
       (c) Where does John live?
       (d) Does John live here?

In (10) the active (a) and passive (b) sentences would have ver
different rewrite rules in a strictly PS grammar, even though
we intuitively consider them to "have the same meaning." In
(11) the three questions (b-d) are all recognized to be related
to the declarative statement (a), yet each would need different
PS rules.

Conversely, there are sentences that appear to use the
same PS rules although we intuitively regard them as having sig
nificant structural differences. The most frequently discussed
such pair is

12) John is easy to please

13) John is eager to please.

n (12) John is the logical object of *please*, whereas in (13)
ohn is the logical subject of *please*. Thus we can have

14)   (a) It is easy (for someone) to please John

      (b) To please John is easy,

ut not

15)   (a) *It is eager (for someone) to please John

      (b) *To please John is eager.[47]

descriptively adequate grammar must account for the fact that
12) and (13) are only superficially similar, as revealed in the
iscrepancy between (14) and (15).

        Ambiguous sentences offer another test case. A much-used
xample is

16) Flying planes can be dangerous.

enerating (16) entirely by PS rules fails to note that the am-
iguity of this sentence can be seen in its relationship to two
ivergent sentences:

17) Flying planes is dangerous

18) Flying planes are dangerous.

escriptive adequacy must reveal the structural differences be-
ween (17) and (18) by further relating (17) to

19) (For someone) to fly planes is dangerous

nd relating (18) to

20) Planes that fly are dangerous.

linguistic theory is needed that can indicate how these two
airs of sentences are related.

        To describe adequately the important PS patterns noted
n (10)-(20) a grammar must employ, in addition to PS rules,
nother type of grammatical rule, the transformation. Such a
rammar is the third model Chomsky discusses, and the one to
hich he devotes his attention. The essential character of a
ransformation rule was presented above as formulated by Zellig
arris. Chomsky developed it considerably further. First he
ontrasted the transformation (T rule) to the PS rewrite rule.
hile the latter always begins with a single symbol, a T rule,
xpressed as $P \Longrightarrow Q$, begins with an entire string (P) and converts
t into another string (Q)[48] by rearrangement, insertion, or de-
etion.[49] From the view of the tree diagram, a T rule maps one

entire phrase-marker "into a new *derived Phrase-marker*."[50] Chom
sky also subcategorized T rules because they can, in addition,
combine two strings into a third string. Zellig Harris labeled
them all simply "grammatical transformations."[51] Chomsky distinguished between the two types by calling the first (converting one string into another) a singulary transformation, and th
second (converting two strings into a third) a generalized tran
formation.[52] Furthermore, Chomsky extended the use of singular
transformation to cover certain obligatory operations. Of most
importance are the affixing of tense and number features to ver
and nouns and the assigning of proper word order in English.
These T rules are obligatory in that they must be applied to a
terminal string before it becomes an acceptable sentence. Such
sentences are the *kernel* sentences of a language. When optiona
T rules are applied additionally, the sentence is a *derived* sen
tence.[53]

   It can be shown that sentences for which PS rules are in
adequate, e.g., (10b), (11b-d), (16), (17) and (18), are in
fact derived sentences, each the result of an optional T rule,
some singulary, such as (10b) from (10a) by a passive transformation, (11b-d) from (11a), each by a different question transformation, and the rest generalized transformations. Consider
again

(16) Flying planes can be dangerous

(17) Flying planes is dangerous

(18) Flying planes are dangerous.

The last one can best be viewed as the result of a nominalizing
transformation involving two strings:

(21)   (a) Planes fly

        (b) Planes are dangerous.

To (21a) is applied an *ing* nominalization, which then replaces
planes in (21b). (17) is likewise derived from two strings:

(22)   (a) They fly planes

        (b) It is dangerous.

The ambiguity of (16) is described as the result of two alternative transformations, the nominalization of either (21a) or
(22a) embedded into

(23) Planes can be dangerous.[54]

These examples demonstrate that a combination of both

phrase-structure generations and transformations is necessary to
account for the important structural features of sentences. We
earlier called this the criterion of descriptive adequacy, the
level of success we are striving for in a grammar. Our subsequent
discussion here will thus presuppose a transformational-generative
(TG) model for grammar.

The view of TG grammar just presented reflects the early
work of Chomsky in *Structures*. The response to this approach,
mostly by his own students, raised a number of issues which led
Chomsky to revise various dimensions of his theory. What is now
called the "standard theory" is presented in *Aspects*.[55] It in-
troduces several significant changes which mainly revolve around
how the grammar is organized and how semantics fits into the
grammar.

The first change is that the PS rules are limited so that
they no longer contain any introduction of vocabulary, i.e., no
more rules such as N —> {boy, girl, . . .}. Rather, the terminal strings which are generated, such as N + V + N, have each
item marked for various features. E.g., N may be marked [+Ani-
mate] [+Human] [-Adult]. The language has a lexicon organized
in a similar way, so that each entry is marked with its appropriate features. Thus "boy" would be marked [+Animate] [+Human]
[+Male] [-Adult], and would be a proper lexical substitute for
the terminal item N, as marked above. The lexicon would likewise mark each verb for the possible features which could be
given to it, e.g., [+Transitive]/__NP, i.e., such a verb could
be used transitively, only in the context where it preceded a
noun phrase. This part of the theory has not yet been worked
out in any detail.[56] The PS rules, or "categorial rules," together with the lexicon, comprise the "base" of the "syntactic
component" of the grammar. The output of the base is a set of
"basic strings." The phrase marker given to each basic string
is called the "deep structure" of that string. It is this "deep
structure" that is interpreted by the "semantic component" which
renders the meaning of the string. Since so little is known
about how the mind handles and organizes semantics, Chomsky did
not spell out the nature of the semantic component; his main
concern was with the syntactic component.

The base, as just described, is only one part of the syntactic component, The other part is the set of transformational rules, which are responsible for changing the highly abstract deep structure of the basic string into a surface structure, which more closely resembles a "sentence" as it is commonly understood (We will shortly illustrate this.) In addition to the syntactic and semantic components, a grammar has a phonological component, which renders the surface structure into an actual utterance. Structuralism had previously done much work with phonology, which Chomsky merely assumed in his grammatical discussion.[57] The relationship of these components has been diagrammed in various ways,[58] of which we offer a modified version:

Syntactic Component

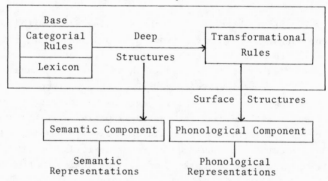

The following is how Chomsky has summarized "the organization of a generative grammar":

A generative grammar must be a system of rules that can iterate to generate an indefinitely large number of structures. This system of rules can be analyzed into three major components of a generative grammar: the syntactic, phonological, and semantic components.
The syntactic component specifies an infinite set of abstract formal objects, each of which incorporates all information relevant to a single interpretation of a particular sentence. . . .
The phonological component of a grammar determines the phonetic form of a sentence generated by the syntactic rules. That is, it relates a structure generated by the syntactic component to a phonetically represented signal. The semantic component determines the semantic interpretation of a sentence. Thus, it relates a structure generated by the syntactic component to a certain semantic representation. Both . . . components are therefore purely interpretive. . .

Consequently, the syntactic component of a grammar must specify, for each sentence, a *deep structure* that determines its semantic interpretation and a *surface structure* that determines its phonetic interpretation. The first of these is interpreted by the semantic component; the second, by the phonological component.

The *base* of the syntactic component is a system of rules that generate a highly restricted (perhaps finite) set of *basic strings*, each with an associated structural description called a *base Phrase-marker*. These base Phrase-markers are the elementary units of which deep structures are constituted. . . . Underlying each sentence of the language there is a sequence of base Phrase-markers, each generated by the base of the syntactic component. I shall refer to this sequence as the *basis* of the sentence that it underlines.

In addition to its base, the syntactic component of a generative grammar contains a *transformational* subcomponent. This is concerned with generating a sentence, with its surface structure, from its basis.[59]

In order for the deep structure to contain all the necessary semantic information, Chomsky had to change his theory of how the transformational rules work. Since the deep strucure must contain all the semantic information, the transformations must be "marked" in the deep structure strings, and thus they become obligatory. That includes both the singulary transformations, such as negative, question, imperative,[60] as well as those that were the generalized transformations. These latter had interrelated two (or more) basic strings. Now such relationships must be shown in the deep structure. Therefore, there is another change in the PS rules which allows the initial sentence symbol, S, to appear on the *right* side of a rewrite rule. Thus the expression "the student who took the course" is generated from the rule NP ⟶ T + N + S' (S "prime" used to indicate a constituent string embedded into the original S, or matrix string). Another feature of *Aspects* is the introduction of an empty terminal symbol, Δ, used when an element in the terminal string has no lexical item inserted into it.

The various matters discussed above can best be further clarified by a base phrase-marker (= the deep structure), variously called Base Marker or Deep Marker, of a carefully restricted English sentence (without lexical feature markings or concord or tense transforms).

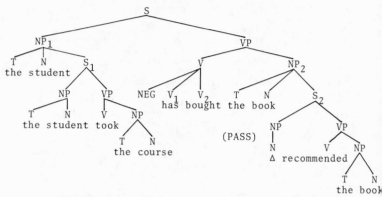

The minimal PS rules for this sentence are:

(24)　(a)　S —→ NP + VP

　　　(b)　NP —→ (T +) N (S')

　　　(c)　VP —→ V + NP

　　　(d)　V —→ (NEG) V_1 + V_2

Traditional functional categories can be described in ter of the grammatical structures of the phrase-marker. The "subje of" S is the labeled node NP directly *dominated by* S, here des-ignated NP_1; the "direct object of" S is the labeled node NP directly dominated by VP, here designated as NP_2. Each of thes two NPs has an embedded S, here labeled S_1 and S_2, which are constituent strings that are embedded into matrix string S. Th relative transformation rule (T_{REL}) transforms S_1 into the string "who took the course," by replacing the identical NP in S_1 with the relative, so NP identity becomes a condition for T_{REL}. This may be formalized as a context-sensitive rule:

(25)　T_{REL}:　NP + VP $\Longrightarrow$

　　　　　　Rel + VP / NP_i.

Spelled out, we have the relative transformation which operates on a basic string NP + VP and transforms it into the string Rel + VP, only in the context of NP identity (the replaced NP is identical with the NP into which S' is embedded).

Before applying T_{REL} to S_2, we note the instruction (PASS to apply T_{PASS} to S_2 first. This requirement of order of T rules is usually called the cyclic principle, wherein all T rul must first be applied to a string for which there are markings in that string before any embed rules are used. The T_{PASS} rule

was given earlier. Applied here the result is "the book was
recommended by Δ." "By Δ" will be deleted by a general rule in
the grammar which deletes all occurrences of Δ (null or empty
terminal elements). So now we have a string that would be equivalent to "the student who took the course NEG has bought the
book which was recommended." The marking NEG requires a T_{NEG}
on the V, vastly over-simplified as

(26) T_{NEG-V}: NEG V_1 + V_2 $\Longrightarrow$
            V_1 + *not* + V_2.

(V_1 is usually labeled Aux [for "auxiliary"].) Finally, after
all the phonological rules have been applied to the string, we
have "the student who took the course has not bought the book
which was recommended." Many details have had to be passed over
as we sought to present only the essence of TG grammar.[61]

The decade following *Aspects* has seen a voluminous body of
literature debating many of the facets of Chomsky's "standard
theory" of TG grammar. Only the two most general and significant
issues can be dealt with here. The first is concerned with the
problem of delineating the semantic component. Rather than
assigning to the semantic component an interpretive role, as
Chomsky does, some of his students have argued that the semantic component really is the initial generative component and
that syntax cannot formally be distinguished from semantics.
Or if it can be, it comes *after* semantics in the organization
of the grammar. The position that suggests that semantics belongs in the base has been labeled "generative semantics." If
semantics generates the base strings, there is no longer any
need to distinguish deep and surface structure, and grammar becomes a linear sequence of components and cyclic operations,
more like the original model of *Structures*, though with different components. There are many nuanced sub-categories in the
general area of generative semantics, all of which is beyond the
scope of our topic. Only Chomsky's outlined reply can concern
us here.

In "Deep Structure, Surface Structure and Semantic Interpretation"[62] Chomsky responds to the various semantic arguments
which were offered against *Aspects*. He considers them attempts
to focus "on the notion of deep structure and the relation of
semantic representation to syntactic structure,"[63] and he offers

evidence for the inadequacy of each response,[64] suggesting that some are "in a sense, mere notational variants."[65] He is more concerned with the "cases in which semantic interpretation seems to relate more directly to surface structure than to deep structure,"[66] especially in English where word order or intonational emphasis can change the focus and other related matters. The question transformation can alter the meaning of a word:

(27)   (a) I shall go downtown

          (b) Shall I go downtown?

as can a negative transformation:

(28)   (a) John will go downtown

          (b) John won't go downtown.

In both cases "shall" and "will" appear to change meaning.[67] After numerous examples, Chomsky concludes

> It seems that such matters as focus and presupposi-
> tion, topic and comment, reference, scope of logical
> elements, and perhaps other phenomena, are determined
> in part at least by properties of structures . . .
> other than deep structures, in particular by properties
> of surface structure.[68]

This revised position Chomsky calls the "extended standard theory" (EST).

The change in EST can be indicated by a modification in the diagram which we gave earlier, into the following EST version (with a line from Surface Structures to Semantic Component):

Syntactic Component

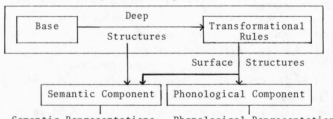

Semantic Representations   Phonological Representations

Later Chomsky dealt with some other "empirical issues" which distinguish EST and generative semantics.[69] There he summarizes:

> The extended standard theory permits only base rules,
> transformational rules, a simple outcondition on sur-
> face structures (and certain other conditions), and
> rules of interpretation applying to deep and surface
> (perhaps also shallow) structures. To be more precise,
> the latter rules apply to phonetically interpreted

surface structures. Furthermore, there are general
conditions on the application of transformations
. . . .

The basic property of transformations is that they
map phrase-markers into phrase-markers. Each transformation applies to a phrase-marker on the basis of
the formal configurations expressed in it, and quite
independently of the meanings or grammatical relations
expressed by these formal configurations.[70]

The label "interpretive semantics" is applied to the semantic
view of EST, in contrast to "generative semantics." Despite
extending his theory, Chomsky maintains that semantics still
plays an interpretive role in a grammar, rather than a generative one. The syntax of a language is not derived from the semantic content of its structures, but is the basis for both the
semantic and phonological output.[71]

The second issue, which chronologically arose first but
has received less discussion, is billed as the "lexicalist position" vs. the "transformationalist position."[72] Though the
lexicalist position is now associated with EST, originally all
TG grammar assumed a tranformationalist position. The issue is
that of the relation between verbs/verbals and derived nominals,
e.g., *refuse/refusing* and *refusal*. The process is called nominalization (T_{NOM}).   The original work was done by Robert B.
Lees.[73] His was the first dissertation completed under Chomsky
(and the first in Linguistics at MIT).[74] Chomsky's original exposition of TG grammar presupposed certain features inherited
directly from Zellig Harris. We have already seen[75] that Harris
considered nominals to be derived from cognate verbs. As Chomsky had initially assumed this stance from Harris, so Lees in
turn also adopted it as the framework for his work on nominalizations.

Lees stated his goal as the study of "that set of rules
by means of which new nouns are created."[76] He took that to
mean *all* nominal constructions which could be thought of as derived from sentences. After summarizing the basic PS rules and
T rules he developed rules for various nominalizations.[77] However, Lees nowhere presents his theoretical rationale for treating derived nominals as transformations, other than the basic
observation that they involve some of the same restrictions on
use as do their cognate verbs.

Chomsky in turn used Lees' *Grammar* in his own further
writings. In a 1962 paper[78] he accepted the transformational
origin of such pairs as
(29)   (a) his refusing to participate
        (b) his refusal to participate
(30)   (a) his rejecting the offer
        (b) his rejection of the offer,
while at the same time noting differences in the two types of
constructions, e.g., the second member of each pair, the "derived nominal," can include adjectives (his *strange* refusal to
participate), but the first, "gerundive," cannot. Two years
later his position appeared to remain the same:

> Clearly, the words *destruction*, *refusal*, etc., will not
> be entered in the lexicon as such. Rather, *destroy*
> and *refuse* will be entered in the lexicon with a fea-
> ture specification that determines the phonetic form
> they will assume . . . when they appear in nominal-
> ized sentences.[79]

Already here, however, he notes some problems involved with this
approach,[80] and in a note[81] suggests an alternative which he was
soon to develop fully into a strong position.

In "Remarks on Nominalization, "[82] Chomsky forcefully argues against his earlier, "transformationalist," stance and opts
completely for a "lexicalist" position. These terms reflect
his statement of the issue: whether to "extend the base rules
to accommodate the derived nominal directly" (through lexical
insertion) or to "simplify the base, excluding these forms, and
derive them by some extension of the transformational apparatus,
insisting that this is not a matter of linguistic theory, but
"entirely an empirical issue."[83]   The differences which he originally noted (some already acknowledged by Lees) between gerun-
dives and derived nominals are here greatly expanded (e.g., ger-
undives are formed much more freely than derived nominals, and
even where they are parallel, they often differ semantically,
so that they cannot be paraphrased in the same way). The two
can be explained differently because of Chomsky's reorganization
of the base of a grammar (discussed above), which separated the
lexicon from the PS rules and assigned contextual features to
lexical entries. Thus he proposes

> as a tentative hypothesis, that a great many items ap-
> pear in the lexicon with fixed selectional and strict

subcategorization features, but with a choice as to the features associated with the lexical categories noun, verb, adjective. The lexical entry may specify that semantic features are in part dependent on the choice of one or another of these categorial features.[84]

Adopting this position involves other consequences. The most immediate is that the PS rules must account for these constructions in the base. If, for example, (29a) and (29b) are generated by separate PS rules as VP and NP, respectively, then noun phrases must be able to generate the same set of components as verb phrases (and adjective phrases). Therefore Chomsky proposed the following rules:

(31) (a) NP —> N Comp

(b) VP —> V Comp

(c) AP —> A Comp

(32) Comp —> NP, S, NP S, NP Prep-P, Prep-P Prep-P, etc.[85]

This formulation of the rules allows for a generalized treatment of all complement constructions, whether used with noun, verb or adjective. Chomsky raises, and then answers, various objections which could be offered against such a position. In summary he states:

It seems that the transformationalist hypothesis is correct for the gerundive nominals [e.g., John's refusing the offer] and the lexicalist hypothesis for the derived nominals [e.g., John's refusal of the offer] and perhaps, though much less clearly so, for the mixed forms [e.g., John's refusing of the offer].[86]

The phenomenon of gerunds has been further investigated more recently by Thomas Wasow and Thomas Roeper.[87] They provide an excellent defense of the lexicalist position by refining gerunds into two classes--nominal and verbal. Verbal gerunds correspond to Chomsky's gerundive nominals, i.e., they are transforms of sentences and thus in the deep structure are directly dominated by S. In constrast, some -*ing* constructions have the internal structure of NP's and so are not transforms at all but lexical items which are directly dominated in the deep structure by NP. Wasow and Roeper list six "specific structural differences" between nominal and verbal gerunds: nominal gerunds (1) "are introduced with articles," (2) "take preceding adjectival modifiers," not "following adverbial modifiers," (3) "can be pluralized," (4) "express the grammatical relation of direct-object-of in a prepositional phrase," not with "the direct object

immediately following the verb," (5) use the negative *no* rather
than *not*, (6) do "not permit a tense marker."[88] These nominal
gerunds function like Chomsky's derived nominals and cannot be
formed freely from all verb stems as can verbal gerunds. Chomsky's third category, "mixed forms," in reality contains both
genuine nominals and verbals which have *of* inserted by analogy
with nominals, and thus "sound considerably more natural if the
preposition *of* is deleted, i.e., if verbal gerunds are substi-
tuted for nominal gerunds."[89]

     In his Extended Standard Theory position Chomsky conjoin
the two issues just discussed (the interpretive and the lexical
ist), in that he presupposes the view of interpretive semantics
when he defends his lexicalist hypothesis, pinning the transfor
mationalist hypothesis to the generative semantics grammarians.

     Within the EST position, the ongoing discussion has take
several different directions, often focusing on details of linguistic theory or on matters specific to the English language
and therefore not of direct interest to our present concerns.
However, one further development in Chomsky's linguistic theory
is directly pertinent to this study: the theory of complementa
tion.

     PS rules (31) and (32) employed the notion of complement
(Comp) as a possible component in the expansion of any major
phrasal node (NP, VP, AP). One of Chomsky's students, Joan
Bresnan, has significantly modified the theoretical approach to
complementation.[90] The theory has gone through several stages
before reaching the form in which it is currently used by Chomsky.[91] Its main feature is the introduction of a new PS rule:
(33) $\bar{S} \longrightarrow$ COMP S[92]
Every embedded S[93] is rewritten COMP (= complementizer, to be
clearly distinguished from the earlier Comp = complement of [31]
and [32]) and S, making COMP a node in the initial phrase-marke
A further PS rule delineates the features of COMP in English:
(34)   COMP $\longrightarrow$ $\left\{ \begin{array}{c} \pm WH \\ for \\ \emptyset \end{array} \right\}$ [94]

+WH is the feature associated with the formation of interrogatives and -WH with non-interrogatives (relative clauses and
that).[95] Certain transformations, such as infinitive, do not

require any lexical realization of COMP, which is represented
by ϕ ("null").

One other central concern in Chomsky's current work is
also the result of one of his students, Joseph Emonds.[96] The
essence of this concern is that transformational operations not
be allowed total freedom to rearrange the structure of a phrase-
marker. In fact, transformations operate within narrow restrictions, or constraints. Emonds argues that there is a general
structure-preserving constraint that operates in all languages,
so that any transformational operation involving a given node
results in an altered phrase-marker that places that node in a
position in which it could have been generated in the initial
phrase-marker. E.g., a transformation that moves an NP must
move it only to a position in which the PS rules could generate
NP. Chomsky's most recent work on transformations[97] has focused
on two features of such movement rules, with the goal of elimi-
nating the need for conditions on the application of transformational rules. The first is his increasingly firm conviction
that *all* transformational rules of the "core grammar" (of English) are of the NP-movement or *wh*-movement type.[98] The second
is that the moved NP or *wh* leaves behind a trace (t) in the position it has vacated. The presence of t is then used by Chomsky as the explanation of how a grammar blocks certain otherwise
unacceptable sequences which would result from the free application of movement rules. Emmon Bach offers a critical analysis
of these two arguments in his response to Chomsky's "*WH*-Movement"
paper,[99] noting that the removal of conditions on transformations
is accomplished at the expense of considerably complicating the
set of necessary "surface" rules and filters. Bach suggests
that these changes really present a significantly different theory,
which he dubs REST ("revised extended standard theory"), in that
it undercuts the original basis for the transformational component in the grammar. Moreover, the movement rules are far too
specific to English to be justified as part of Universal Grammar.
The theory of trace, however, merits serious consideration within the earlier framework of movement rules as one typical feature
of transformations.[100]

In the analysis which follows we will adopt Chomsky's EST,
including his interpretive semantics and lexicalist positions,

as modified by his current discussion of complementation and
general structure-preserving constraints. The lexicalist position is especially important because we will concentrate our
study on nominalizations and interpret that to *exclude* derived
nominals. We will also accept the Wasow and Roeper distinction
between nominal and verbal gerunds (though we call them parti-
ciples).

        Since the transformations we are studying often involve
NP nodes, the movement constraint is an important restriction
to observe in the formulation of our transformational rules.
However, working with a language that uses inflection more than
word order, we cannot limit transformations to movement rules.

CHAPTER THREE

TRANSFORMATIONAL RULES FOR NOMINALIZATIONS
IN HELLENISTIC GREEK

In the previous chapter we sketched the development of
Chomsky's transformational-generative (TG) approach to syntax.
While the goal of his linguistics is to arrive at the features
of Universal Grammar (UG), the actual work was done on English
and therefore the results often take the shape of rules for English grammar. As these rules are debated and reformulated in
the literature, new levels of understanding are achieved about
UG, which in turn affects the formulation of new rules of English. So each continues to have its direct influence on the
other as both are being investigated. Linguists are still far
from writing even an outline of either a TG English grammar or
UG; but in the meantime the results of the work already done on
TG grammar has begun to be applied to many other languages.[1]

In our survey of the study of Hellenistic Greek (HG) grammar, we saw that work was just getting underway using structuralist linguistics when the TG revolution began. During the
twenty years since then no significant work has yet been written
on HG grammar using TG linguistics.[2] However, during the past
five years a Hellenistic Greek Linguistics Project has been en-
gaged in research directed toward that goal.[3] The Project has
in progress *An Outline of a Transformational-Generative Grammar
of Hellenistic Greek*,[4] which we will use as the overall framework within which to investigate nominalizing transformations.
We will also adopt its notational symbols (given in Appendix I).

Nominalizations are transformations which embed sentences
into noun phrases, or, put less formally, they are the syntactic
devices which allow an embedded sentence (traditionally, dependent clause) to function nominally. Embedded sentences can also
function adnominally and adverbially. All of this can be

41

expressed as part of a set of basic PS rules:[5]

(1) (a) $S \longrightarrow$ NP [AUX] VP

(b) NP $\longrightarrow$ $\begin{Bmatrix} N\ (\bar{S}) \\ \bar{S} \end{Bmatrix}$ (adnominal)

(c)   (nominal)

(d) VP $\longrightarrow$ V (Adv)

(e) Adv$\longrightarrow$ $\begin{Bmatrix} NP \\ \bar{S} \end{Bmatrix}$

(f)   (adverbial)

(g) $\bar{S} \longrightarrow$ COMP S

Embedding transformations have to do with (1b), (1c), and (1f),
yielding, respectively, adnominalizing transformations or adnom-
inalizations, nominalizing transformations or nominalizations
and adverbializing transformations or adverbializations. Any
embedding transformation thus implies rule (1g), meaning that
the embedding is accomplished through the use of COMP as its embedding device. If COMP is not realized as a complementizer-wor,
then embedding is achieved morphologically by means of either a
participle (Vpt) or an infinitive (Vif). For ease of reference
we will refer to this method of embedding as non-COMP. In fact,
we can incorporate non-COMP into rule (1g) as (1g'):

(1) (g') $\bar{S} \longrightarrow$ ±COMP S

with +COMP realized as the presence of a complementizer-word
and -COMP realized as a morphological element in the embedded
S, in the case of Greek attached to the verb.

We can indicate these various possibilities also in the
form of a phrase marker (PM):

(2)

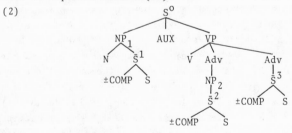

The matrix sentence (S^o) has three embeds: 1) $\bar{S}^1$, functioning
adnominally; 2) $\bar{S}^2$, functioning nominally; and 3) $\bar{S}^3$, functionir
adverbially. We could also have put the nominal embed ($\bar{S}^2$) unde
NP_1 and the adnominal construction (N $\bar{S}^1$) under NP_2; i.e., any
NP can have either an adnominal or nominal embed, regardless of

where in the structure the NP is. In contrast, an adverbial embed, by definition, can only be in VP; therefore we make the
distinction between $\bar{S}^2$ and $\bar{S}^3$ by the presence of NP_2.

This study then will focus on the combination of (1c)
NP $\longrightarrow$ $\bar{S}$ and (1g') $\bar{S}$ $\longrightarrow$ ±COMP S (e.g., $\bar{S}^2$), to determine the
embedding process in HG for nominalized embeds: When are +COMP
and -COMP chosen? How is that choice related to the function
of the NP node into which S is embedded? And, what are the actual embedding transformations in each case?

We will begin with nominalizations that use a complementizer-word, i.e., the feature +COMP. The most frequent nominalizing COMP is ὅτι (it is also the second most frequent COMP
in general, next to the adnominalizing COMP ὅς).

Here are examples of its nominalizing uses in the New
Testament:

(3) (a) Jn 11:20 ἤκουσεν ὅτι ᾽Ιησοῦς ἔρχεται
                   She heard that Jesus was coming

     (b) Mk 2:1   ἠκούσθη ὅτι ἐν οἴκῳ ἐστίν
                   It was reported that he was at home

     (c) Jn 4:1   ἔγνω ὁ ᾽Ιησοῦς ὅτι ἤκουσαν οἱ Φαρισαῖοι ὅτι
                   . . . .
                   Jesus knew that the Pharisees had heard that
                   . . . .

(4) (a) Jn 9:20   οἴδαμεν ὅτι οὗτός ἐστιν ὁ υἱὸς ἡμῶν
                   We know that this is our son

     (b) Mk 6:49   ἔδοξαν ὅτι φάντασμά ἐστιν
                   They thought that it was a ghost

     (c) Jn 11:27 ἐγὼ πεπίστευκα ὅτι σὺ εἶ ὁ χριστός
                   I believe that you are the Christ

     (d) Jn 6:24   εἶδεν ὁ ὄχλος ὅτι ᾽Ιησοῦς οὐκ ἔστιν ἐκεῖ
                   The crowd saw that Jesus was not there

     (e) Heb 13:18 πειθόμεθα ὅτι καλὴν συνείδησιν ἔχομεν
                   We are convinced that we have a clear con-
                   science

(5) (a) Mk 4:38   οὐ μέλει σοι ὅτι ἀπολλύμεθα;
                   Don't you care that we are perishing?
                   Doesn't it concern you that we are perishing?

     (b) Gal 3:11 ὅτι ἐν νόμῳ οὐδεὶς δικαιοῦται παρὰ τῷ θεῷ
                   δῆλον
                   It is clear that no one is justified before
                   God by the law

(c) 1 Cor 1:11 ἐδηλώθη μοι . . . ὑπὸ τῶν Χλόης <u>ὅτι</u> ἔριδες
ἐν ὑμῖν εἰσιν

It has been made clear to me . . . by
Chloe's people that there is strife among
you

(6) (a) Ac 21:31 ἀνέβη φάσις τῷ χιλιάρχῳ . . . <u>ὅτι</u> ὅλη συγχύν
νεται Ἰερουσαλήμ

A report reached the commander . . . that al
Jerusalem was in an uproar

(b) Phil 2:22 τὴν δοκιμὴν αὐτοῦ γινώσκετε, <u>ὅτι</u> . . . ἐδοὐ
λευσεν . . . .

You know his character, that . . . he serve
. . . .

(c) 1 Jn 5:11 αὕτη ἐστὶν ἡ μαρτυρία, <u>ὅτι</u> ζωὴν αἰώνιον ἔδα
κεν ἡμῖν ὁ θεός

The witness is this: God has given us eter
nal life

(d) Rom 6:6 τοῦτο γινώσκοντες, <u>ὅτι</u> . . . .

Knowing this, that . . . .

(e) Ac 4:13 ἐπεγίνωσκον αὐτοὺς <u>ὅτι</u> σὺν τῷ Ἰησοῦ ἦσαν

They recognized them, that they had been with
Jesus

(7) (a) Ac 20:38 εἰρήκει <u>ὅτι</u> οὐκέτι μέλλουσιν τὸ πρόσωπον
αὐτοῦ θεωρεῖν

He had said that they would never see his
face again

(a') Ac 20:25 ἐγὼ οἶδα <u>ὅτι</u> οὐκέτι ὄψεσθε τὸ πρόσωπόν μου

I know that you will never see my face agair

(b) Mk 6:18 ἔλεγεν ὁ Ἰωάννης τῷ Ἡρῴδῃ <u>ὅτι</u> οὐκ ἔξεστίν c

(b') Mt 14:4 ἔλεγεν ὁ Ἰωάννης αὐτῷ οὐκ ἔξεστίν c

John had said to Herod, "It is not lawful for
you"

(c) Jn 18:8 ἀπεκρίθη Ἰησοῦς εἶπον ὑμῖν <u>ὅτι</u> ἐγώ εἰμι

Jesus answered, "I told you, 'I am'"

(c') Jn 18:5 λέγει αὐτοῖς ἐγώ εἰμι

He said to them, "I am"

(d) Jn 14:28 ἠκούσατε <u>ὅτι</u> ἐγὼ εἶπον ὑπάγω

"You heard me say, 'I go away'"

The sentences in (3) all have the verb ἀκούω (I hear).
In each case ὅτι marks the beginning of the nominal embed; i.e.
the ὅτι-clause is functioning as an NP, the same as would a lex
ical NP. Compare (3a) with (3a'), this time employing limited
bracketing:

(3)   (a) Jn 11:20   ἤκουσεν [$_{\bar{S}}^{NP}$ [$_{COMP}$ὅτι] [$_S$ ᾿Ιησοῦς ἔρχεται]]

      (a') Ac 5:24   ἤκουσαν [$_{NP}$ τοὺς λόγους τούτους]

                     (They heard these words)

In (3a') the NP node is filled with a lexical NP, which then
becomes accusative (in the final morphological transformational
cycle) because of its function in relation to the verb, whereas
in (3a) the NP is rewritten as S̄, which in turn is rewritten
COMP and S. It is noteworthy here that S retains its original
present tense, even though embedded into a matrix clause that
is past tense, in contrast to English, which requires a sequence
of tenses that changes the embedded S into past tense. So in
Greek, S is able to function nominally solely with the use of
+COMP —> ὅτι, an embedding device that cannot change morphologically.

        To further demonstrate that the S̄ in (3a) functions as
does the NP in (3a'), we note that it is acceptable to apply a
passive transformation (T_{PASS}) to either one, giving sentences
analogous to (3b) and (3b'):

(3)   (b) Mk 2:1   ἠκούσθη [$_{\bar{S}}^{NP}$ [$_{COMP}$ὅτι] [$_S$ ἐν οἴκῳ ἐστίν]

      (b') Ac 11:22 ἠκούσθη [$_{NP}$ ὁ λόγος].

                     (The report was heard)

In (3b') a structure similar to (3a') has undergone T_{PASS},
resulting in NP now functioning as subject, i.e., moved in the
phrase marker to the position of NP dominated by S and eventually
given nominative form, and V now marked for passive. When the
same T_{PASS} is applied to a structure like (3a) to yield (3b),
the V is again marked passive and the NP again becomes the dominant NP, functioning as subject. However, the nominalizing
transformation (T_{NOM}) remains the same as in (3a): +COMP —>
ὅτι, and S is unaffected, including its tense. So our initial
formulation of T_{NOM} is (T_1) T_{NOM}: +COMP —> ὅτι.

        The next example

(3)   (c) Jn 4:1   ἔγνω ὁ ᾿Ιησοῦς [$_{\bar{S}}$ ὅτι ἤκουσαν οἱ Φαρισαῖοι

                   [$_{\bar{S}}$ ὅτι....]]

shows that this nominalizing process is cyclic, i.e., a sentence
like (3a) can itself be embedded as a nominal into another sentence. Such repeated embedding was described in the previous
chapter as recursive right-embedding,[6] since the process of
adding an embedded sentence *after* the matrix is repeated within
the embed itself.

The examples in (4) above are indicative of other sentences with similar nominalizations in the VP. In each case S̄
again has +COMP ⟶ ὅτι and S in its original tense, which can
be different from that of the matrix verb, as in (4b) and (4d).
Another similarity of all the sentences in (3) and (4) is that
all the matrix verbs are of the same type, sometimes called per-
ception verbs. They might better be called verbs of "cognition"
hear, know, think, believe and see (the list could be extended--
recognize, confess, understand, argue, remember). A distinctive
feature of these verbs is that the content of whatever the verb
"cognizes" may be expressed as a nominalization embedded with
ὅτι. Though there is no agreed upon appropriate label for this
verb-type or verb-class, TG linguistics has long recognized the
need for subcategorizing verbs according to the kinds of embedding transformations that occur with them.[7] These verbs would
be marked in the lexicon for their subcategorization and selec-
tion features,[8] e.g.,

(L_1) [+____ [$_{COMP}$ ὅτι] [S]]

would indicate, in the description of a verb, that it is acceptable (+) for this word to be inserted in the context ____ ὅτι
S. Most ὅτι nominalizations do, in fact, occur in an NP that
is dominated by VP of this class of verbs.[9] The most common ver
of this class is the saying-verb λέγω/εἶπον, which will be
treated separately below.

Nominalizations can also occur in an NP that is dominated
by S, i.e., functioning as subject (in its initial phrase marker), though the possible constructions here are more limited.
In

(5) (a) Mk 4:38 οὐ μέλει σοι [$^{NP}_{S}$ [$_{COMP}$ ὅτι] [$_S$ ἀπολλύμεθα]]

the embedded sentence is a nominalization functioning as the
subject of an "impersonal" verb. This class of verbs is marked
in the lexicon for the selectional feature (L_2):

(L_2) [+[$_{NP}$S̄] ____ [$_{NP}$ +HUMAN]]

indicating that this word is an acceptable lexical insert into
a PM that has S̄ as its dominant NP and as its adverbial NP a
lexical noun with the feature +HUMAN. What makes the construction "impersonal" is the nominalization functioning as subject,
with the "personal" NP as an adverbial (in the dative case).
Furthermore, both German and English, the languages in which the

standard grammars are written, have a stylistic transformation
often used in such sentences that moves the "that/*dass*" clause
(nominalization) to the end of the sentence, leaving an empty
initial NP that is then filled by "it/*es*," thereby emphasizing
the "impersonal" content of the NP functioning as subject.

The other impersonal constructions with ὅτι are similar
to (5b):

(5) (b) Gal 3:11 $[_S^{NP} [_{COMP}$ ὅτι] $[_S$ ἐν νόμῳ δικαιοῦται...]] δῆλον.
The ὅτι-embed again comprises the entire dominant NP, but the
VP consists of a neuter singular adjective, sytactically analyzed as an equative VP with the equative (lexically empty) verb
deleted (indicated in the deep structure by Δ=). The stem δηλ-
also occurs in the verbal form δηλόω and is found in Attic in
the "impersonal" construction δηλοῖ μοι ὅτι....,[10] directly parallel to (5a), and also analogous to (5b). So the stem δηλ- has
the lexical features of (L_2) regardless of whether it appears
in the sentence as (lexically) a verb or an adjective. This is
consistent with the lexicalist position described in the previous
chapter.[11] Constructions of this type are far less common than
those with the earlier feature (L_1). Μέλει is the only such verb
to gain currency in Greek (see also Lk 10:40) and the primary
other adjective besides δῆλον (see 1 Cor 15:27 and πρόδηλον in
Heb 7:14) is φανερόν (see also Ac 4:16). There are other "impersonal" verbs and adjectives, but they use infinitive embeds
and thus will be discussed later.

Also in the category of ὅτι-embeds as subject is (5c):
(5) (c) 1 Cor 1:11 ἐδηλώθη μοι ... ὑπὸ τῶν Χλόης $[_S^{NP}$ ὅτι....]
which is further related to (5b) in that the matrix VP in each
is built on the same lexical stem: δηλ-. However, the verb form
in (5c) is passive, so in the deep structure the ὅτι-embed is
not the dominant NP, but an adverbial NP in the VP, like the
ὅτι-embeds in (3)-(4). Therefore (5c) is really more akin to
(3b) *structurally*, though it *lexically* resembles (5b), and in
its surface structure it is an "impersonal" construction like
(5a). The same pattern exists for φανερόν and its corresponding
passive verb (see 2 Cor 3:3 and 1 John 2:19). The apparent similarity of (5c) to both (5a) and (5b), and to (3b), results from
the combined features of ἐδηλώθη: 1) its stem is δηλ-, therefore
it has the same lexical features as (5b); 2) it is an --δω verb,

and thus adds a "causative," or better, "factitive"[12] feature to
a structure like (5b), making the embed function adverbially as
its "content" clause, which therefore gives it a deep structure
similar to (3b); however, 3) the passive transformation is then
applied, making the embed again function as subject, corresponding to (5a).[13]

    We have been discussing the function of nominalizations
according to the NPs into which they are embedded. Some are embedded into an NP that is part of VP (functioning adverbially)
and others are embedded into NP dominated by S (functioning as
subject). There is yet a third syntactic position for an NP,
and that is in apposition to another NP, which can be indicated
by NP<Ap>NP, with both NPs having the same syntactical function
(and therefore in the same case), though not having any direct
syntactic link. Appositive NPs occur often with names and title
('Ἰησοῦς ὁ Ναζωραῖος; 'Αγρίππας ὁ Βασιλεύς) or with personal pro
nouns (ἐγὼ Παῦλος; ὑμεῖς οἱ Φαρισαῖοι), but they can also be use
as in (6a):

(6)   (a) Ac 21:31 ἀνέβη [$_{NP}$ φάσις]... [$_S^{NP}$ ὅτι...]

The ὅτι-embed is a nominalization functioning appositively with
the dominant NP of the sentence. The relation between the two
NPs is not made any more explicit in the surface structure.
However, the nouns that are found with appositive ὅτι-embeds are
based on stems that share the "cognition" feature which we associated with the verb-class that is used with ὅτι-embeds. In bot
cases the most common type is the verb/noun of speaking (λέγω/
εἶπον; λόγος/ῥῆμα). We will discuss these in more detail below
when we consider direct discourse.

    The ὅτι-embed in (6b)

(6)   (b) Phil 2:22 [$_{NP}$τὴν δοκιμὴν αὐτοῦ] γινώσκετε [$_S^{NP}$ ὅτι....]

is in apposition to an NP that does not have the "cognition"
feature; however, the matrix verb is a member of the verb-class
which has that feature, suggesting that, in the hierarchical
structure, both NPs are directly dominated by the VP, as well
as being in apposition to each other. This also argues against
any deep structure explanation which initiates all appositives
as equative sentences, since the two NPs in (6b) are able to be
in apposition only because each one is independently an acceptable insertion into this VP, not because, put together, the

two would be an acceptable equative sentence. Further evidence
is seen in Paul's use of the formula οὐ θέλω ὑμᾶς ἀγνοεῖν, which
is followed directly by a ὅτι-embed in Rom 1:13 and 1 Cor 10:1,
but in Rom 11:25 the ὅτι-embed is in apposition to another NP,
τὸ μυστήριον τοῦτο, an adverbial NP in the accusative case. The
verb involved, ἀγνοέω, is used by Paul with either an NP accusative (Rom 10:3; 2 Cor 2:11) or a ὅτι-embed (Rom 2:4; 6:3; 7:1),
i.e., it is a member of the "cognition" verb class which is fea-
ture-marked for both constructions, and thus it is acceptable
in this VP to use the two together in apposition. (Similar examples are in 2 Cor 9:2; Eph 3:2-3; Jas 5:11.)

The most common appositive construction is a ὅτι-embed in
apposition to a demonstrative determiner (traditionally called
a demonstrative pronoun), either in an equative sentence like
(6c) or in a "cognition" VP like (6d). In (6c)

(6)   (c) 1 Jn 5:11 [$_{Dd}^{NP}$αὕτη] ἐστὶν [$_{NP}$ἡ μαρτυρία] [$_{\bar S}^{NP}$ὅτι....]

it is not self-evident which of the first two NPs is functioning
as subject nor to which one the ὅτι-embed is in apposition.[14]
This particular sequence, Dd + V= + NP + S̄, is typically Johannine (ten times with αὕτη alone). The use of αὕτη ἐστίν elsewhere, however, suggests a different initial structure, similar
to (6c'):

(6)   (c') 1 Cor 9:3 [$_{NP}$ἡ ἐμὴ ἀπολογία]...ἐστὶν [$_{Dd}^{NP}$αὕτη]:
                      [$_{\bar S}^{NP}$μη...;]

(My reply . . . is this: Don't we have...?)
indicative of the non-Johannine uses (Ac 8:32; 2 Cor 1:12; Jas
1:27). Thus we take the third NP in both (6c) and (6c') to be
in apposition to αὕτη, which in the Johannine style is placed
first. We also note that the dominant NP in each is formed from
a lexical stem (μαρτυρ-, ἀπολογ-) which belongs to the "cognition" verb class. So the syntax of the ὅτι-embed in (6c) is
the same as in (6a). For the same reason the ὅτι-embed in (6d)

(6)   (d) Rom 6:6 [$_{Dd}^{NP}$τοῦτο] γινώσκοντες [$_{\bar S}^{NP}$ὅτι...]

has the same syntax as in (6b). The two NPs are in apposition,
but each one is an acceptable insert into a VP with the feature
markings of the ("cognition") matrix verb.

An extension of the construction just discussed in (6b)
and (6d) is found in (6e):

(6)   (e) Ac 4:13 ἐπεγίνωσκον [$_{NP}$αὐτοὺς] [$_{S}^{NP}$ὅτι...ἦσαν].

In the surface structure the two NPs appear to be in apposition.
However, the embedded sentence has as its dominant VP an NP
identical to the preceding lexical NP. Grammars traditionally
describe this as ὅτι preceded by the subject of its clause. The
linguistic explanation offered by TG grammar for the analogous
infinitive construction is that the NP involved is *raised* from
its position in the embed to a position in the matrix VP.[15] Apparently in Greek such a movement rule is permitted in VPs that
have "cognition" verbs, i.e., their adverbials can be either a
lexical NP or a ὅτι-embed. When the ὅτι-embed occurs, its dominant NP can optionally be moved into the adverbial position of
a lexical NP, leaving the rest of the ὅτι-embed unaffected.
Since in Greek the embedded verb retains the person and number
marking of the dominant NP, even if it is not filled lexically,
removing the "subject" NP does not change the syntax of the embedded sentence. Most instances of this phenomenon involve personal pronouns, which only occur as dominant NPs when emphatic,
so in (6e')

(6) (e') Mt 25:24 ἔγνων [$_{NP}$σε] [$^{NP}_S$ὅτι σκληρὸς εἶ ἄνθρωπος][16]

it is not surprising that σε is omitted in some manuscripts (D
Θ 46 1207 1391), in effect nullifying the raising transformation
nor that Luke uses a different matrix verb (ἐφοβούμην) which
makes ὅτι causal and not a nominalization.[17] (Likewise, it is
not a transformation used in English with *that*-constructions,
but only with infinitives.) This raises some doubt about the
status of the raising transformation with ὅτι-embeds, but we
can say that the reason it is possible at all is because of the
feature markings on "cognitive" verbs, and that where it occurs
it is not an appositive construction but a raising transformation
from an embed of the type we saw in (4).

The one factor common to all the sentences in (6) is that
the "cognition" marking is present on the lexical stem that is
directly related to the appositive embed. In (6b), (6d) and
(6e) it was a feature of the matrix verb, as in (3)-(4) above.
In (6a) and (6c) the lexical stem with this marking was the noun
in apposition to the embed. Again, as in (5) above, this explanation is offered within the lexicalist position, wherein the
feature markings on a lexical stem are common to whatever verbal
or nominal forms it takes.

We have postponed the discussion of one of these stems, or actually subgroup of stems, until we saw the features of the rest of the class. Our discussion now will focus on the use of ὅτι-embeds with λέγω and εἶπον. The λέγω/εἶπον construction most analogous to those in (4) is so-called indirect discourse. Compare (7a) and (7a'):

(7) (a) Ac 20:38 εἰρήκει [$_S^{NP}$ὅτι [$_S$οὐκέτι μέλλουσιν τὸ πρόσωπον
                                        αὐτοῦ θεωρεῖν]]

     (a') Ac 20:25   [$_S$οὐκέτι ὄψεσθε τὸ πρόσωπόν μου]

The S embedded by ὅτι in (7a) refers to the direct statement made in (7a'), however both the first person pronoun and the second person marking on the verb are changed to the third person, making this an indirect reference to the statement given directly in (7a'). When an original statement is quoted directly, first and second person features are retained, as in (7b), and ὅτι is deletable, as in (7b'):

(7) (b) Mk 6:18 ἔλεγεν [$_{NP_1}$τῷ 'Ηρῴδῃ] [$_S^{NP}$ὅτι [$_S$οὐκ ἐξεστίν
                                                      [$_{NP_2}$σοι]]]

     (b') Mt 14:4 ἔλεγεν [$_{NP_1}$αὐτῷ]   [$_S$οὐκ ἐξεστίν
                                                      [$_{NP_2}$σοι]]]

Matthew's deletion of ὅτι in (7b') in contrast to Mark in (b) is rather typical,[18] suggesting that Matthew and Mark reflect different rules for deleting ὅτι in direct discourse. Thus it is likely that there are rules that will explain the various constructions in which each author deletes ὅτι with direct discourse, but the formulation of such rules requires analysis beyond the scope of this study. The clearest case, offered here as an example, seems to be in John, especially in the use of εἶπον.

      Consider again (7c) and (7c'):

(7) (c) Jn 18:8 ἀπεκρίθη 'Ιησοῦς [$_{S^1}$εἶπον ὑμῖν [$_S$ὅτι [$_{S^2}$ἐγώ
                                                         εἰμι]]]

     (c') Jn 18:5   λέγει αὐτοῖς   [$_S$ἐγώ εἰμι]

In (7c) the answer given in S^2 is the repetition of something that had already been said, in (7c'), but now ὅτι is used to mark what was originally the direct discourse, the S of (7c'). This suggests that John uses ὅτι as equivalent to our printing convention of single quotation marks within double quotation marks. This is much more restricted that the common adage that

ὅτι functions simply as optional quotation marks in Greek discourse. However, scribes did not always understand John's limited use of ὅτι and often treated it as though it were more freely deletable. We will note this along with the evidence for the
Johannine use of εἶπον ὅτι in direct discourse as follows:

Original Statement	Repeated in Dis- course with ὅτι	ὅτι Omitted[19]
1:48	1:50	Byz Θ f¹ pl
4:17a	4:17b	(made indirect in D)
6:30	6:36	
8:21	8:24	
[9:7	9:11	P⁷⁵ A D Byz W Γ Δ Θ Λ Π X f¹ f¹³ pl]²⁰
11:25	11:40	P⁶⁶ 69
8:21	13:33	P⁶⁶ ℵ* D W 579 pc
16:14	16:15	
18:5	18:8	

There are also some instances when the repeated statement
with ὅτι is introduced by narrative rather than by other direct
discourse:

Original Statement	Repeated in Nar- rative with ὅτι	ὅτι Omitted
9:21	9:23	
13:10	13:11	ℵ A Byz Γ Δ Θ f¹ f¹³ pm
17:12	18:9	

While the εἶπον ὅτι construction in Johannine discourse
appears to be limited to introducing repeated statements (4:52;
5:15; 7:42 and 21:23 are indirect discourse; and 8:55 and 14:2
are hypothetical discourse with ἄν),²¹ it is not used in every
such situation. The analogous examples which do not use ὅτι are
limited to constructions where the εἶπον itself is part of an
embed that is embedded with +COMP (often ὅτι).

    Compare (7c) to (7d):

(7)   (c) Jn 18:8 ἀπεκρίθη [s̄¹[COMP₁___][s¹εἶπον [s̄²[COMP₂ ὅτι]
                                              [s²....]

      (d) Jn 14:28 ἠκούσατε [s̄¹[COMP₁ ὅτι][s¹εἶπον [s̄²[COMP₂___]
                                              [s²....]

In constructions like (7c) the direct discourse COMP ($COMP_1$) is always deleted in John, in contrast to the ὅτι in $COMP_2$, which embeds repeated discourse within direct discourse. However, in constructions like (7d) $\bar{S}^1$ is embedded with +COMP, in which case the COMP of repeated discourse ($COMP_2$) is deleted.

The examples are:

Original Statement	Repeated in Embedded Discourse Without ὅτι	ὅτι Inserted
1:15[22]	(ὅς) 1:30	
3:3	(ὅτι) 3:7	
1:20	(ὅτι) 3:28	p[66],[75] 700 pc
4:50	(ὅς) 4:53	Byz D W Θ 078 f[1] al[23]
7:34	(ὅς) 7:36	P[66] pc
8:21	(ὅτι) 8:22	
10:30,33	(ὅτι) 10:36	
14:4,18	(ὅτι) 14:28	
13:16	(ὅς) 15:20	
16:16	(ὅς) 16:17	
16:16	(ὅτι) 16:19	
18:5	(ὡς) 18:6	

The above evidence suggests that the Johannine rule for ὅτι with εἶπον in direct discourse is: in the DELETION cycle, when "Delete Direct Discourse ὅτι" is applied, ὅτι is deleted only if its dominating $\bar{S}$ is itself part of another $\bar{S}$ embedded by +COMP, i.e., in the Johannine stylistic rules for direct discourse, the deletion of ὅτι in $COMP_2$ is blocked when $COMP_1$ is empty.

We have examined various nominalizations embedded with ὅτι. We have seen that the basic nominalizing transformation is apparently +COMP $\longrightarrow$ ὅτι. We further discovered that there are only two contexts in which this occurs: 1) as the dominant NP, functioning as subject of "impersonal" constructions, which is limited to only a few lexical stems, and 2) primarily as adverbial and appositive NPs, related to lexical stems of one type, which we called "cognition." Such stems can become either verbs having ὅτι-embeds as adverbial NPs, or nouns having ὅτι-embeds as appositives.

These limitations all have to do with the matrix sentence into which the nominalization is embedded. We need finally to

consider the nature of the embeds themselves. Another look at
the ὅτι-embeds in (3)-(7) reveals that the S̄ which is embedded
is in each case a declarative sentence, to the exclusion of both
commands and questions.

The use of command forms (imperative and hortatory subjunctive) in embedded constructions is limited to direct discourse, where the ὅτι is deleted. In our discussion of the Johannine stylistic rule for ὅτι with repeated discourse, we noted
that where ὅτι would otherwise seem to be required, it is absent
when the embed is a command.[24] There are in fact no instances
in HG of a command in a ὅτι-embed. Blass-Debrunner cites a "hor
tatory subjunctive" and an "imperatival ἵνα" in the New Testament, and an imperative in a fourth-century papyrus,[25] though
none of these is a direct discourse ὅτι introducing a command.
The "hortatory subjunctive" in Rom 3:8 is functioning simultane-
ously within two different syntactical constructions. It is
first of all asked as a rhetorical question introduced by μή
(parallel to v. 5), but it also relates to the parenthetical
statement which Paul inserts between μή and the subjunctive
(. . . καθὼς φασίν τινες ἡμᾶς λέγειν ὅτι). Whatever the role
of ὅτι is in the relationship between the parenthetical clause
and the rhetorical hortatory subjunctive, it has more to do with
the style of Pauline parentheses than it does with the ὅτι-embeds. Likewise, the "imperatival ἵνα" in Mk 12:19 is involved
in a complex construction. It is part of a modified Septuaginta
quote, preceded by a compound conditional clause, with ὅτι as
part of the formula introducing the scriptural quote. Thus this
is less an example of an imperatival ὅτι-embed than it is of a
Marcan introduction of Scripture. Finally, there is an imperative as a ὅτι-embed in P Oxy 1683.20, a "late fourth-century,"
"very illiterate letter."[26] The letter writer does use ὅτι
(ὤτι) before an imperative form, but he is explicitly repeating
an earlier conversation and therefore using ὅτι in the Johannine
style with repeated discourse, though without the Johannine restrictions which delete this ὅτι with imperatives and within
another +COMP embed. However, this same author ("illiterate"
for his phonetic spelling) elsewhere deletes ὅτι before an imperative when it gives the content of a "cognition" verb, but
uses it to embed a declarative with such a verb,[27] reflecting

a careful nominalizing use of ὅτι, which includes deletion with
imperative, but not with repeated discourse.

Another cause for deleting ὅτι within direct discourse is
when the embed is a question. Again we will briefly look at the
counter-examples and the problems involved with each. The primary examples are Mk 4:21 and 8:4. The manuscript evidence for
reading ὅτι in each passage is limited, respectively, to B L 892
and B L Δ, all from the same (Alexandrian) text-type. Since the
Nestle editions are based largely on Codex B, they print ὅτι in
both these passages.[28] We have noted that ὅτι before direct
discourse tends to be unstable in scribal hands,[29] so with the
evidence limited here to one text-type, it is quite possible
that we have two more instances of a scribal addition of "optional quotation marks," and not a case for direct discourse
ὅτι before questions. Blass-Debrunner cites: Rom 10:15 P⁴⁶
γέγραπται ὅτι πῶς. . . .[30] A close examination of the manuscript, however, indicates that the reading is ὅτι ὡς.[31] Since
the ὡς is part of the scriptural quotation, and is exclamatory,
we have another instance of scribal addition of ὅτι with direct
quotation and not a direct question at all. Therefore we conclude that ὅτι is deleted in direct discourse when the embed is
a direct question, as well as when it is a direct command. Whatever the stylistic rule may be for an author's use of ὅτι in direct discourse, it does not include using it with commands and
questions. Thus the use of ὅτι in direct discourse is the same
as it is with any nominalization: ὅτι is the +COMP which embeds
a declarative sentence into an NP which functions either adverbially in a "cognition" VP or appositively to a "cognition" NP.

Non-declarative sentences (commands and questions) are
embedded by means other than ὅτι. We will look next at ἵνα, the
second most common nominalizing complementizer in HG. Here are
New Testament examples of its nominalizing use:

(8)   (a) Mk 6:8 παρήγγειλεν αὐτοῖς ἵνα μηδὲν αἴρωσιν
                 He ordered them not to take anything
      (b) Lk 10:40 εἰπὸν αὐτῇ ἵνα μοι συναντιλάβηται
                 Tell her to help me
      (c) 1 Cor 16:12 παρεκάλεσα αὐτὸν ἵνα ἔλθῃ πρὸς ὑμᾶς
                 I urged him to visit you

(d) Mt 27:32 τοῦτον ἡγγάρευσαν <u>ἵνα</u> ἄρῃ τὸν σταυρόν

They forced this man to carry the cross

(9) (a) Jn 11:50 συμφέρει ὑμῖν <u>ἵνα</u> εἷς ἄνθρωπος ἀποθάνῃ ὑπὲρ τοῦ λαοῦ

It is advantageous for you that one person should die for the people

(b) Mt 10:25 ἀρκετὸν τῷ μαθητῇ <u>ἵνα</u> γένηται ὡς ὁ διδάσκαλος αὐτοῦ

It is enough for the student to be like his teacher

(10) (a) Jn 13:34 ἐντολὴν καινὴν δίδωμι ὑμῖν <u>ἵνα</u> ἀγαπᾶτε ἀλλήλο

I give you a new commandment: love one anoth

(b) Ac 27:42 τῶν στρατιωτῶν βουλὴ ἐγένετο <u>ἵνα</u> τοὺς δεσμώτας ἀποκτείνωσιν

The soldiers' plan was to kill the prisoners

The patterns of sentences in (8), (9) and (10) are very analogous to (4), (5) and (6), i.e., we are working with the same sets of phrase markers, so we will analyze ἵνα-embeds in terms similar to the ὅτι-embeds. Each ἵνα-embed in (8) is a nominalization embedded into an NP which is functioning adverbially in a VP that has a certain type of matrix verb. We call the verb-class in (4) "cognition" verbs. In (8) the verbs are again all of one class: order, tell, urge, compel (and this li could also be expanded: e.g., command, request, proclaim.)[32] We will call them verbs of "exhortation." They are the class o verbs marked in the lexicon for the selectional feature (L_3): (L_3): [+___ [$_{COMP}$ἵνα] [S]].
This suggests that the transformation involved is simply +COMP- ἵνα. However, we saw with ὅτι-embeds that the S embedded by th ὅτι is always declarative, so we must next consider the type o S which is embedded by ἵνα.

Compare (8a) with (8a'):

(8) (a) Mk 6:8 παρήγγειλεν αὐτοῖς [$_S$[$_{COMP}$ἵνα] [$_S$μηδὲν αἴρωσιν]]

(a') Lk 9:3 εἶπεν πρὸς αὐτούς,   [$_S$μηδὲν αἴρετε]

In (8a) the S has a verb marked for subjunctive and in the thi person. In (8a') Luke has put the same sentence into direct discourse as a command, with the verb marked for imperative an in the second person. The sentence underlying the S in (8a') thus the same sentence underlying the S in (8a). The change i the verb form from second person to third person is part of th change from direct to indirect discourse, as with the declarat

mbed in (7a). There is another change here, however, from im-
erative form to subjunctive form, that indicates the presence
f an additional feature marking in the embed. The additional
arking is best explained as a modal marking, a feature of the
UX (Auxiliary) node,[33] indicated in (1a) by [AUX].

A sentence in imperative form results from the transfor-
ation of a deep structure with a modal marking for *Command*, the
trongest modality of VOLITION. When the S with the *Command* mar-
ing is an embed, that feature marking in its AUX node affects
he embedding transformation in two ways: 1) the choice of +COMP
an no longer be ὅτι, but must be a "modal" COMP, which is pri-
arily ἵνα, and 2) the embedded verbal form is marked for sub-
unctive. Thus the choice of the ἵνα-subjunctive construction
s a nominalization is explained as the transformation of the
command marking in the embedded S. We already said above that
uch a nominalized S̄ functions adverbially in a VP that has an
"exhortation" verb, and now we can characterize that embed as
he "content" of the exhortation. This is the common feature
f all the sentences in (8).

The sentences in (9) have a nominalized embed functioning
s the dominant NP. Like the sentences in (5), these are con-
tructions which have a matrix VP with a lexical stem that has
he "impersonal" selectional feature (L_2), i.e., συμφέρει with
να is analogous to μέλει with ὅτι, and like δηλ-, the stem ἀρκ-
an be used in impersonal constructions either as a verb (ἀρκεῖ,
ee Jn 14:8, without an embed, but conjoined to an imperative)
r as an adjective, as in (9b). The difference between (9) and
5) is that the embedded sentences in (9) have a modal marking
or VOLITION and therefore are embedded by +COMP ⟶ ἵνα, with
he embedded verb marked for subjunctive. However, it is less
bvious than in (8) what the gradient of the modal marking is.
n (9a):

9) (a) Jn 11:50 συμφέρει ὑμῖν [$_{\bar{S}}$[$_{COMP}$ἵνα][$_{S}$εἷς ἀποθάνῃ]
he S has a verb marked for a modality that is usually trans-
ated into English as "should," and could be paraphrased as
"ought to," which are both degrees of VOLITION. However, in the
ollowing verse John explains to the reader that the speaker of
9a) was prophesying that Jesus ἔμελλεν ἀποθνῄσκειν, suggesting
hat the modal marking of S in (9a) is now transformed into

μέλλω, which is usually an aspectual marking ("about to"). Jo
uses it again with ἀποθνῇσκειν in 12:33 (and 18:32), which in
turn is interpreted in the next verse as δεῖ, a modal marking
strong POSSIBILITY, which seems to be the Johannine mode in al
these references to Jesus' death. Therefore it is not possibl
to claim the same special modal marking for all ἵνα-embeds.
Since there is no scholarly consensus on what the categories o
modality are,[34] it is best to use a more general label like
"strong modal" to cover all cases of nominalized embeds that u
ἵνα for +COMP.

The sentences in (10) have ἵνα-embeds as appositives to
matrix NPs. The lexical stem involved in each matrix has the
same "exhortation" feature marking as the matrix verbs in (8)
(See Jn 11:53; 12:10; 15:17.) This is analogous to the patter
we saw in the lexical stems of (4) and (6), i.e., whether the
nominalizations function adverbially or appositionally, if the
are ἵνα-embeds, they have a "strong modal" marking and they ar
embedded into an "exhortation" context.

Closely associated with the ἵνα-subjunctive constructio
is ὅπως-subjunctive. Compare (11a) and (11b):

(11) (a) Lk 11:37 ἐρωτᾷ αὐτὸν Φαρισαῖος ὅπως ἀριστήσῃ παρ' αὐ
          A Pharisee asked him to dine with him

      (b) Lk 7:36 ἠρώτα τις αὐτὸν τῶν Φαρισαίων ἵνα φάγῃ μετ'
          αὐτοῦ
          One of the Pharisees asked him to eat with

As in (11a) the few other examples of ὅπως as a nominalizing
COMP are also with verbs of "asking" and found mostly in Luke-
Acts (Lk 7:3; 10:2; Ac 8:15,24; 23:20; 25:3; elsewhere in
Mt 8:34; 9:38; Jas 5:16). It appears to be a relic of Attic
that is losing its currency because ἵνα is becoming the standa
COMP for modal embeds. It may be that ὅπως was originally the
COMP for embeds with a modal marking "less strong" than that o
the ἵνα-embeds (with verbs of "asking" rather than "exhorting"
but such a distinction was not maintained by most users of HG,
with even Luke using ἵνα in (11b) as a stylistic variation of
ὅπως in (11a). This was part of the process that gained such
stronghold for ἵνα as the dominant "modal" COMP in HG.[35] We c
clude, therefore, that the nominalizing transformation for ἵνα
must indicate that it is contextually restricted to the presen
of a modal marking (+M) in the embed, which we formulate as T_2

T_2) T_{NOM}: +COMP ⟶ ἵνα/+M.

This is the T_{NOM} used primarily for embedding "strong modals"
into "exhortation" VPs. Among the "exhortation" verbs are verbs
of "asking" with the sense of "requesting," especially ἐρωτάω,
as in (11b). However, when a VP has a verb of "asking" with
the sense of "questioning," and the embed is an embedded (indirect) question, the verb is in a different verb-class than "exhortation" and the nominalization is also different.

We turn next, then, to embedded questions, beginning again
with several sets of examples:

(12) (a) Lk 16:4 ἔγνων <u>τί</u> ποιήσω   see 16:3 τί ποιήσω;
               I know what I will do

      (b) Jn 1:39 εἶδαν <u>ποῦ</u> μένει   see 1:38 ποῦ μένεις;
               They saw where he was staying

      (c) Jn 5:13 οὐκ ᾔδει <u>τίς</u> ἐστιν   see 5:12 τίς ἐστιν...;
               He did not know who it was

(13) (a) 1 Jn 3:2 οὔπω ἐφανερώθη <u>τί</u> ἐσόμεθα
               It is not yet clear what we shall be

      (b) Mk 1:24 οἶδά σε <u>τίς</u> εἶ
               I know who you are

The sentences in (12) all contain embedded questions that
are given as direct questions in the preceding verse. The syntactic sequence of the sentences is the very same as with the
embedded "declaratives" in (4), namely a VP with a "cognition"
verb and a complementizer introducing an embed with an "indicative" verb form. In (12) the COMP position is filled by the
question word, in English WH-words and in Greek Π-words. The
direct question form of the embedded questions indicates that
it is the question transformation itself (which is outside the
scope of our study) that moves the Π-word to the initial position in the sentence, called Π-fronting.[36] When the sentence with
the question (Q) marker is an embed, then the Π-fronting of the
question transformation (T_Q) moves the Π-word into COMP. Thus,
in the transformational cycle for embedding, COMP is already
filled, so any additional transformation is blocked.

In (13) are two examples further indicating the analogous
position of Π-embeds to ὅτι-embeds. (13a) has the Π-embed functioning as the subject of an "impersonal" passive construction,
exactly parallel to (5c),[37] and (13b) is an instance of "raising"

the deep structure pronominal "subject" (second person singular)
into the position of an adverbial NP in the matrix VP, exactly
parallel to (6e).[38]

This evidence suggests that the only distinction between
ὅτι-embeds and Π-embeds is that the latter are embedded sentences
that have Q markers, necessitating the application of T_Q *before*
the embedding transformation and therefore blocking any other
realization of +COMP. All other features of these two sets of
embeds are the same. Thus we cannot really talk about a separate nominalizing transformation for "questions." Rather, the
are "índicatives" like ὅτι-embeds, but with Q markers, in contrast to ἵνα-embeds as "non-índicatives."[39]

Two other matters related to embedded questions can be
mentioned only briefly. The first is the use of certain adnom
inal embeds which appear to be very similar to Π-embeds.[40]

(14) (a) Mk 4:24 βλέπετε [$_S^{NP}$τί ἀκούετε]

      Heed what you hear

      (b) Mt 11:4 ἀπαγγείλατε [$_{NP}$ΔN [$_S^{A}$ἃ ἀκούετε]

      Report what you hear

In (14a) the S̃ is an embedded question as in (12). However, t
S̃ in (14b) is an adnominal embedded by a relative complementiz
(ἃ) into an NP which has a deleted (lexically empty) noun, som
times called a "headless relative clause." Thus the transformation involved in (14b) is an adnominalization and not a nomi
nalization, and we are not considering such constructions in
our study. It is important to note that Greek distinguishes
between these two types of embedding devices: Π-words moved i
to COMP position and ὅ-words[41] as complementizers, whereas bot
are WH-words in English.[42]

The second matter has to do with embedding other kinds
questions. Questions involving Π-words are only one type of
question transformation. The other type is the Yes/No, or non
Π-word question, i.e., a Q marker when there is no Π-word, as
in (15a):

(15) (a) Mk 15:2 ἐπηρώτησεν αὐτὸν ὁ Πιλᾶτος, σὺ εἶ ὁ Βασιλεὺς
                   τῶν ᾿Ιουδαίων;

                   Pilate asked him, "Are you the king of the
                   Jews?"

and therefore there is no word to be "fronted." Consequently,
the transformation does not alter the position of any element

in S, so only the speaker's intonation indicates the presence of
the Q marker. When such a Yes/No question is an embed, as in
(15b):

(15)   (b) Mk 15:44 ἐπηρώτησεν αὐτὸν <u>εἰ</u> πάλαι ἀπέθανεν

                 He asked him if he had already died

it has a complementizer (εἰ) which is neither a Π-word nor a ὅ-
word.[43] The εἰ-COMP also occurs in direct questions, as in (15c):

(15)   (c) Ac 5:8 εἰπέ μοι, <u>εἰ</u> τοσούτου τὸ χωρίον ἀπέδοσθε; ἡ δὲ
              εἶπεν, ναί, τοσούτου

              Tell me: did you sell the land for so much?
              She said, "Yes, for so much."

The fact that the εἰ-construction in (15c) is responded to with
a direct affirmative answer suggests that it is a direct Yes/No
question. Indeed, most of the "indirect" εἰ questions in the
New Testament appear to fit this category.

      As part of the Yes/No transformation the εἰ in (15c) func-
tions to provide the Yes/No "fronting" which is lacking in
(15a).[44] This is analogous to question transformations which
are marked for their expected answer by "fronting" with οὐ when
expecting "Yes" and by μή when expecting "No," as in (15d):

(15)   (d) Jn 7:41-2 οἱ δὲ ἔλεγον, μὴ ἐκ τῆς Γαλιλαίας ὁ χριστὸς
              ἔρχεται; οὐχ ἡ γραφὴ εἶπεν . . . ἀπὸ Βηθ-
              λέεμ . . .;

              Some said, "The Messiah doesn't come from
              Galilee, does he? Doesn't Scripture say
              . . . from Bethlehem . . .?

Questions with οὐ- and μή-marked answers are not used as embeds
in the New Testament, i.e., there are no εἰ οὐ or εἰ μή embedded
questions, though there are a few extant examples elsewhere.[45]

      We have been considering the +COMP embedding transforma-
tions in HG. We can summarize them by the association of COMP
with type of embedded sentence: 1) with índicative modal marking
either a) +COMP is ὅτι, or b) the índicative has a Q marker,
which either i) moves a Π-word into COMP position, blocking the
+COMP transformation, or ii) the Q marker is realized as εἰ and
fronted like a question word, again blocking +COMP; 2) with non-
índicative modal marking +COMP is ἵνα and the modal marking is
realized as the subjunctive form of the embedded verb.

      We formulated the embedding rule (1g') as

(1) (g') S̄ ⟶ ±COMP S

and we have seen the several realizations of +COMP when S̄ is a

nominalization. We will now consider the -COMP realizations of
nominalizing transformations. The only frequent -COMP nominalization is that which results in the infinitive form of the embedded verb. The infinitive embed (Inf-embed) is used in the
following nominalizations:

(16) (a) Jn 12:18 ὅτι ἤκουσαν [$_S^{NP}$ τοῦτο αὐτὸν πεποιηκέναι]

              Because they heard (that) he had done this

      (b) Lk 4:41 ὅτι ᾔδεισαν [$_S^{NP}$ τὸν χριστὸν αὐτὸν εἶναι]

              Because they knew (that) he was the Messiah

      (c) Ac 12:9 ἐδόκει [$_S^{NP}$ ὅραμα βλέπειν]

              He thought (that) he was seeing a vision

      (d) Ac 15:11 πιστεύομεν [$_S^{NP}$ σωθῆναι]

              We believe (that) we are saved

      (e) Lk 20:6 πεπεισμένος ἐστὶν [$_S^{NP}$ Ἰωάννην ποφήτην εἶναι]

              They are convinced (that) John is a prophet.

     The matrix verbs in (16) are all the same "cognition"
verbs[46] that we saw in (3)-(4) with ὅτι-embeds, and the S̄ in
each case has the same syntactical function as the corresponding
S̄ in (3)-(4). This suggests that the Inf-embed is the -COMP
equivalent to the ὅτι-embed as a +COMP transformation, i.e., the
two appropriate realizations of ±COMP S. Then the choice betwee
+COMP and -COMP in this situation is not contingent upon any
deep structure feature, but is rather a choice made in a later
cycle as part of the embedding transformation. We will call it
a "stylistic" choice.

     Stylistic choices are made for a variety of reasons. In
(16a) and (16b) the VP into which S̄ is embedded is itself part
of a (causal) ὅτι-embed, suggesting that Inf was chosen to avoid
using ὅτι again. Stylistic choices are often also a reflection
of an author's preference, e.g., (16b-e) are all from Luke-Acts,
with (16b) a Lucan addition to Mark and (16e) parallel to a ὅτι-
embed in Mk 11:32.[47]

     Inf-embeds are also used with "saying" verbs:

(17) (a) Mk 12:18 λέγουσιν [$_S^{NP}$ ἀνάστασιν μὴ εἶναι]

              They say (that) there is no resurrection

      (b) Jn 12:29 ἔλεγεν [$_S^{NP}$ βροντὴν γεγονέναι]

              They said (that) it had thundered

Each S̄ in (17) is an índicative S that could have been transformed also into a ὅτι-embed, analogous to (7a).

A more common pattern, however, is the use of Inf-embeds with "exhortation" verbs:

(18)   (a) Lk 8:56 παρήγγειλεν αὐτοῖς [$_S^{NP}$μηδενὶ εἰπεῖν]
              He ordered them not to tell anyone
       (b) Lk 12:13 εἰπὲ τῷ ἀδελφῷ μου [$_S^{NP}$μερίσασθαι]
              Tell my brother to share
       (c) 2 Cor 2:8 παρακαλῶ ὑμᾶς [$_S^{NP}$κυρῶσαι . . . ἀγάπην]
              I urge you to reaffirm . . . your love
       (d) Lk 8:38 ἐδεῖτο αὐτοῦ . . . [$_S^{NP}$εἶναι σὺν αὐτῷ]
              He begged him . . . to be with him

The sentences in (18a-c) are exactly parallel to (8a-c), with the same matrix verbs, each with an S̄ giving the "content" of the exhortation,[48] but in (8) each S̄ was a ἵνα-embed with a subjunctive verb form. We concluded that these constructions were transformations of modal markings in the S̄, which we labeled "strong" VOLITION. This holds true for (18) also. (18a) is Luke's parallel to the ἵνα in Mk 5:43, as is Lk 9:21 to Mk 8:30, and the Inf-embeds with παραγγέλλω in Lk 5:14 and 8:29 are parallel to imperatives in Mark. In fact, Luke always uses Inf-embeds with this verb (another ten times in Acts), a clear "stylistic" preference for infinitive over ἵνα-embeds.

In (18d) Luke has a "request" verb with Inf-embed, parallel to his "request" verbs in (11) with ὅπως and ἵνα. Luke uses δέομαι with all three (Inf: Lk 9:38; Ac 26:3; ὅπως: Lk 10:2; Ac 8:24; ἵνα: Lk 9:40; 21:36; 22:32; in addition to four times with direct discourse). Thus Inf is a "stylistic" choice in place of ὅπως-subjunctive, as well as in place of ἵνα-subjunctive. The difference between choosing a -COMP (Inf) and a +COMP (ἵνα) transformation, is that the "strong" modal marking in S̄ is transformed with +COMP into a subjunctive marking on the embedded verb, but when -COMP transforms the verb into a "moodless" infinitive form, no subjunctive marking is possible, so apparently the modal marking of the embed is lost. However, the matrix verb is an "exhortation" verb, which itself has "strong" volitional features in its lexical "meaning," suggesting that once the modality of the sentence is marked, a second occurrence of the same marking is deletable, since the "meaning" of the sentence (however its "semantic representation"[49] is determined and formalized) is unaffected.

The Inf-embeds in (16)-(18) have covered all the categories of nominalizations functioning adverbially that we looked a
as +COMP embeds. The other two categories we considered were
"subject" nominalizations and appositives. The infinitive tran
formation (T_{INF}) is also used with such constructions:

(19)　(a) Jn 18:14　συμφέρει [$_S^{NP}$ἕνα ἄνθρωπον ἀποθανεῖν ὑπὲρ τοῦ
　　　　　　　　λαοῦ]

　　　　　　　It is advantageous for one person to die on
　　　　　　　behalf of the people

　　　(b) Mt 3:15　πρέπον ἐστὶν ἡμῖν [$_S^{NP}$πληρῶσαι πᾶσαν δικαιοσύ-
　　　　　　　　νην]

　　　　　　　It is fitting for us to fulfill all righteous
　　　　　　　ness

　　　(c) Mt 15:20　[$_S^{NP}$τὸ ἀνίπτοις χερσὶν φαγεῖν] οὐ κοινοῖ τὸν
　　　　　　　　ἄνθρωπον

　　　　　　　To eat with unwashed hands does not defile a
　　　　　　　person

　　　(d) Jas 1:27　θρησκεία καθαρὰ . . . αὕτη ἐστίν [$_S^{NP}$ἐπισκέπ-
　　　　　　　　τεσθαι ὀρφανοὺς . . . .]

　　　　　　　Pure religion . . . is this: to visit or-
　　　　　　　phans. . . .

The constructions in (19a-b) are analogous to the "imper
ative" ἵνα-embeds in (9a-b). In fact, (19a) is a repeat of th
earlier direct statement in (9a). In our discussion of (9a) w
concluded that its S̄ was marked for "strong modal," and sugges
ted that in John this would more likely be a "strong" POSSIBIL
ITY marking than a "strong" VOLITION marking. If (19a) is a
stylistic variation of (9a), we again have the loss of the modal marking, as in (18). There we suggested that the matrix
verb had a "strong modal" feature as part of its lexical "mean
ing," making the embedded modal marking deletable. If that ap
plies to this "impersonal" construction, it would suggest that
verbs like συμφέρει are semantically marked for "modality," an
therefore likely candidates to become "modal verbs." This cou
well be the origin of δεῖ ("it is needful/necessary" = "must
as the modal transformation for *Necessity*, e.g., Mt 24:6 δεῖ
γενέσθαι, "this must happen." Thus συμφέρει is also beginning
to function the same way,[50] e.g. Mt 19:10 οὐ συμφέρει γαμῆσαι,
"he should not marry." Likewise, in (19b) πρέπον is from a le
ical stem with similar "modal" features, i.e., πρέπει is on it
way to becoming the Modern Greek for "must," having largely re
placed δεῖ in that capacity.

The Inf-embed in (19c) is also functioning as a dominant NP, but in a matrix S that is not an "impersonal" construction. In (19d) the Inf-embed is a nominalization in apposition to a demonstrative determiner, as are the ὅτι-embeds in (6c-d), but we saw there that the dominant stem in the matrix construction was a member of the "cognition" verb class that was characteristic of ὅτι-embeds. Here the dominant stem (θρησκεία) is not a member of such a lexical class. Thus (19c) and (19d) indicate that the Inf-embed is used in nominalizations that function in constructions not limited to the "cognition" and "exhortation" categories of the ὅτι- and ἵνα-embeds, respectively.

The pattern that has emerged here for the infinitive as a nominalization is 1) it is an equivalent transformation to ὅτι for embedding S̄ into "cognition" phrases; 2) it is an equivalent transformation to ἵνα for embedding S̄ into "exhortation" phrases; and 3) it is used to embed S̄ into other unrestricted phrases. The infinitive, therefore, is the most freely applied nominalizing transformation. It is the only nominalization that can be chosen for all three categories, and thus it does not have a characteristic trait corresponding to the (+COMP) ὅτι and ἵνα transformations. As a -COMP transformation, it is lacking a complementizer, the most obvious feature of +COMP. Furthermore, lacking a COMP, its embedding device is the "moodless" infinitive form, which blocks any additional modal marking, depriving Inf of yet another distinctive +COMP feature.

SUMMARY AND CONCLUSIONS

In our first chapter we looked at the study of Hellenistic Greek grammar during the past two centuries. All the standard grammars of the modern era have been written during that period. That was also a period of several momentous revolutions in linguistic theory. Each new understanding of the nature of language and how to study it was eventually applied to Hellenistic Greek. However, a significant new development had each time out-dated the results just as they were beginning to gain currency, and the "lag-time" in the twentieth century has increased even more.

Beginning with Winer, the first major New Testament Greek grammar, we noticed its strong rationalist emphasis and its understanding of the living, spoken language of the New Testament. The comparative philologists were quick to set aside "rational grammar" for the study of the historical progression of morphology in related languages. As the methodology of nineteenth century historical-comparative linguistics was being applied to the study of HG grammar by the scholars whose works are still standard today, that very approach was replaced with the structuralist linguistics which dominated the first half of this century. Before any lasting structuralist work was done on HG grammar, however, the discipline of linguistics was completely redefined by Noam Chomsky's theory of transformational-generative grammar. TG linguistics has significantly revolutionized the understanding, study and teaching of language, as well as influenced various other fields. Of the few areas that have remained relatively untouched by this revolution, two of the more noticeable are classics and biblical studies, which share Greek grammar in common. This study has endeavored to begin correcting that.

The second chapter presented the basic development of Chomsky's TG linguistic theory, beginning with its outgrowth from structuralism. We then outlined the issues that gave rise to

the "extended standard theory" and in particular to the interpretive and lexicalist positions, as presuppositions for our
own investigation of nominalizations. We also considered some
of the more recent TG discussions that are pertinent to the understanding of nominalizing transformations, especially the theory of complementation, the formulation of embedding rules and
the conditions on transformations.

In the third chapter we applied this TG understanding of
syntax to a study of nominalizing transformations in Hellenistic
Greek. We formulated the basic embedding rule as (1g'), repeate
here as (20a):

(20)   (a) $\bar{S} \longrightarrow \pm COMP$ S.

We began with +COMP embeds and saw that there are basically two
realizations of +COMP in nominalizations, which we can formulate
as (20b-c):

(20)   (b) +COMP $\longrightarrow$ $\begin{Bmatrix} \text{ὅτι/-M} \\ \text{ἵνα/+M} \end{Bmatrix}$
       (c)

i.e., ὅτι in the context of índicative modal marking (-M), and
ἵνα with non-índicative (+M) (which also undergoes a further,
modal transformation into a subjunctive verb form). We also
noted that each of these is limited to certain matrix contexts,
i.e., (20b) into a matrix phrase marked for the lexical feature
"cognition," and (20c) marked for "exhortation."

The primary alternative nominalizing transformation is
(20d):

(20)   (d) -COMP $\longrightarrow$ Inf

i.e., the transformation is realized as the "moodless" infinitiv
form of the verb. While (20d) can be used as an option for either (20b) or (20c) it is not limited to such a feature marking
in the matrix phrase. We suggested that the choice between such
options is properly the area of "stylistics."

In the course of our analysis we noted that embedded ques
tions are a sub-set of (20b), where $\bar{S}$ has a Q marker, which when
transformed blocks ὅτι. We saw that ὅπως was a sub-set of (20c)
used for a limited area of "exhortation." (20b-d) are also used
as the "subject" embeds for certain "impersonal" constructions,
and we suggested that the "impersonal verbs" which use (20d) for
embedding may, in fact, explain the origin of "modal verbs."

This analysis of nominalizations has opened up various areas which need further investigation. The understanding of "style" as related to the pattern of transformational choices has direct bearing on how "style" is used as evidence for many critical methodologies. For example, it has affected our approach to textual criticism (pp. 52, 55); it has influenced the translations of our example sentences throughout the last chapter (see also n. 21); it has provided a way to discern a pattern in an author's writing style (pp. 53, 62). There are also many other areas where "linguistic evidence" is cited as a criterion for making evaluations regarding texts, sources, forms, authorship,[1] interpretation, and more fundamentally, the very understanding of the nature of human language. Wherever this applies to material written in Hellenistic Greek, we have offered an indication of how transformational-generative grammar can further that understanding.

NOTES - INTRODUCTION

[1]Lars Rydbeck, "What Happened to New Testament Greek Grammar after Albert Debrunner?" *New Testament Studies* 21 (1975) 424-27.

[2]For a more popular treatment of many of the issues discussed in that chapter see Noam Chomsky, *Language and Responsibility*. Based on conversations with Mitsou Ronat. Translated from the French by John Viertel (New York: Pantheon, 1979).

NOTES - CHAPTER ONE

[1]This view is championed by Noam Chomsky, especially in *Cartesian Linguistics* (New York: Harper and Row, 1966) and in *Language and Mind* (New York: Harcourt, Brace and World, 1968).

[2]First published in 1660 and now in reprint: *Grammaire Générale et Raisonée, ou La Gammaire du Port-Royal*, by Claude Lancelot and Antoine Arnauld, ed. Herbert H. Brekle (Stuttgart-Bad Canstatt: Friedrich Frommann, 1966). For a lengthy review of the Brekle edition see Robin Lakoff (*Language* 45 [1969] 343-64), who argues that its philosophical basis precedes Descartes, and in fact is motivated by the work on Latin of the 16th century Spaniard, Sanctius. A new English translation, based on Brekle's edition, has recently been published: *General and Rational Grammar: The Port-Royal Grammar*, eds. Jacques Rieux and Bernard E. Rollin (The Hague: Mouton, 1975), with preface, introduction and critical essay which give helpful historical information and discuss Chomsky's Cartesian evaluation of the Grammar.

[3]Gottfried Hermann, *De emendanda ratione Graecae grammaticae* (Leipsig: Gerhard Fleischer, 1801).

[4]George B. Winer, *Grammatik des neutestamentlichen Sprachidioms* Leipsig: Vogel, 1822). Winer produced six editions by the 1850's, after which Gottlieb Lünemann enlarged it for a seventh edition in 1867. Editions 1, 4, 6, and 7 were translated into English. The sixth edition (1855, Winer's last) was translated initially by Edward Masson, *A Grammar of the New Testament Diction* (Edinburgh: T. & T. Clark, 1859[1]; 1863[4]) and then revised by William F. Moulton, *A Treatise on the Grammar of New Testament Greek* (Edinburgh: T. & T. Clark, 1870[1]; 1882[3]), incorporating the material left by Winer. This last edition will be cited as Winer-Moulton. An American revision of Masson was also made, based on the seventh edition of Lünemann, translated by J. Henry Thayer,

A Grammar of the Idiom of the New Testament (Andover: Warren
Draper, 1869).   A new (eighth edition) German revision was begun, but never finished, by Paul Schmiedel (Göttingen: Vandenhoeck & Ruprecht, 1894-98).

[5]Winer was aware of only one New Testament Greek grammar
earlier than his: "George Pasor [d. 1637] . . . left amongst
his papers a N.T. Grammar, which was published with some addi-
tions and corrections of his own, by his son Matthias Pasor . .
under the title *G. Pasoris Grammatica Graeca Sacra N.T. in tres
libros distributa* (Groning. 1655, pp. 787).   This work is now
a literary rarity . . ." (Winer-Moulton, 5).

[6]See the discussion in the references in n. 1 and n. 2.

[7]Winer-Moulton, xxi.

[8]Ibid., 1-3.

[9]Ibid., 7-9.

[10]Ibid., 20-21.

[11]His detailed investigations on the Egyptian Greek papyri
are brought together in Adolf Deissmann, *Light from the Ancient
Near East*, tr. by L. R. M. Strachan (New York: George H. Doran,
1910; reprinted, Grand Rapids: Baker, 1978).

[12]Franz Bopp, *Ueber das Konjugationssystem der Sanskritsprache* (Frankfurt-am-Main, 1816), later developed into a complete *Vergleichende Grammatik* (1833-1852).

[13]Friedrich Blass, *Grammatik des neutestamentlichen Griechisch* (Göttingen: Vandenhoeck & Ruprecht, 1896); *Grammar of New
Testament Greek*, tr. by Henry St. John Thackeray (London: Macmillan, 1898).

[14]Ibid., 1.

[15]Although not to the same extent as by Alexander Buttmann
whose New Testament grammar originated as an appendix to his father's classical Greek grammar, but was translated as a separate
volume (intending to be more concise than Winer).   See Alexander
Buttmann, *A Grammar of the New Testament Greek*, tr. J. Henry
Thayer (Andover: Warren Draper, 1873).

[16]It is interesting to note that already in his first edition, Blass expressed disinterest in the direction which linguistics was taking.   In his preface (untranslated by Thackeray
"on account of the somewhat personal character given to it,"
[See n. 13]), Blass explained to his mentor that because of his
attachment to classical "philology" [*Philologie*], he was not
able to follow the direction taken by comparative "linguistics"
[*Sprachforschung*], usually also called "philology"].   This distinction is indicative of the attitude of classical philologists
to the new course set for comparative philology in the 1870's by
the *Junggrammatiker* ("neo-grammarians"), who focused on the detailed changes in the phonology and morphology in Indo-European

languages.   The nature of the debate is beyond the scope of our
study, but it is summarized in most introductory texts on linguistics, e.g., John Lyons, *Introduction to Theoretical Linguistics* (Cambridge: Cambridge University, 1968) 28-33.

[17] Friedrich Blass and Albert Debrunner, *A Greek Grammar
of the New Testament and Other Early Christian Literature*, tr.
Robert W. Funk (Chicago: University of Chicago, 1961).

[18] Ibid., ix.

[19] Friedrich Blass and Albert Debrunner, *Grammatik des neutestamentlichen Griechisch*, ed. Friedrich Rehkopf (Göttingen:
Vandenhoeck & Ruprecht, 1976).

[20] James H. Moulton, *A Grammar of New Testament Greek*, vol.
I: *Prolegomena* (Edinburgh: T. & T. Clark, 1906[1]; 1908[3]), and
most of the work for vol. II.

[21] James H. Moulton and Wilbert F. Howard, *A Grammar of New
Testament Greek*, vol. II: *Accidence and Word-Formation* (Edinburgh:
T. & T. Clark, 1929; parts i and ii were published in 1919 and
1920), hereafter cited as Moulton-Howard.

[22] James H. Moulton, *A Grammar of New Testament Greek*, vol.
III: *Syntax*, by Nigel Turner (Edinburgh: T. & T. Clark, 1963),
hereafter cited as Moulton-Turner.   The comment is from Turner's
Preface, v.

[23] James H. Moulton, *A Grammar of New Testament Greek*, vol.
IV: *Style*, by Nigel Turner (Edinburgh: T. & T. Clark, 1976),
hereafter cited as Moulton-Turner, *Style*.

[24] Moulton, *Prolegomena*, x-xi.

[25] Ibid., 1-2.

[26] Ibid., 4.

[27] Ibid., 18-19. Moulton's commitment to this assertion is
demonstrated in the other great project he began: James H. Moulton and George Milligan, *The Vocabulary of the Greek Testament
Illustrated from the Papyri and Other Non-Literary Sources* (Grand
Rapids: Eerdmans, 1930; reprinted 1974). Milligan's General Introduction discusses Moulton's support of Deissmann and the an-
ticipations of that view in the 19th century. Milligan's primary example of "Deissmannism before Deissmann" is Masson's
Prolegomena to his translation of Winer's Grammar (see n. 4),
where Masson does indeed talk about the language of the New Testament as "unaffected Hellenic," but Milligan never mentions
Winer's own position in that very volume (which we presented
above).

[28] Moulton-Howard, vi-vii, 413-16.

[29] Moulton-Turner, 1.

[30] Ibid., 2-5.

[31] Ibid., 9.

[32] Moulton-Turner, *Style*, 2-3.

[33] Moulton, *Prolegomena*, xvi (in the "Note to the Third Edition," where he responded to "some leading critics of Deissmannism").

[34] See above, n. 25.

[35] In the 1919 reprint of the third edition of vol. I, quoting James Hastings, editor of *Expository Times*, on the page facing the title page.

[36] A. T. Robertson, *A Grammar of the Greek New Testament in the Light of Historical Research* (Nashville: Broadman, 1914[1]; 1923[4]; reprinted, 1934).

[37] Ibid., vii.

[38] Ibid., 8.

[39] Karl Brugmann, *Griechische Grammatik*, Handbuch der Klassischen Altertums-Wissenschaft II.1 (Munich: Beck, 1890[2]; 1913[4] ed. Albert Thumb), the work of one of the "neo-grammarians" mentioned in n. 16.

[40] Robertson, *A Grammar of the Greek New Testament*, viii.

[41] Ibid., 41. Note also the full title of the *Grammar*.

[42] Ibid., 379.

[43] Ibid., ix.

[44] Ferdinand de Saussure, *Cours de Linguistique Générale*, eds. Charles Bally and Albert Sechehaye (Paris: Payot, 1916); English title: *Course in General Linguistics*, tr. Wade Baskin (New York: McGraw-Hill, 1959). For a discussion of de Saussure impact see David Crystal, *Linguistics* (Baltimore: Penguin, 1971) 158-67, and Lyons, *Introduction to Theoretical Linguistics*, 38-52.

[45] Note the many similarities to Winer above.

[46] Leonard Bloomfield, *Language* (New York: Henry Holt, 1933).

[47] Franz Boas, ed., *Handbook of American Indian Languages* ("Smithsonian Institution: Bureau of American Ethnology," Bulletin 40; Washington: Govt. Printing Office, 1911-1938). Boas may be considered the founder of the "American school" of linguistics.

[48] Best typified in the work of Zellig Harris (see the discussion in the next chapter).

[49] Charles C. Fries, *The Structure of English: An Intro-duction to the Construction of English Sentences* (New York: Har-court, Brace, 1952), a study of English syntax based on a cor-pus of recorded conversations.

[50] Paul Roberts, *Understanding Grammar* (New York: Harper & Row, 1954); *Patterns of English* (New York: Harcourt, Brace, 1956); *Understanding English* (New York: Harper & Row, 1958).

[51] Paul Roberts, *English Sentences* (New York: Harcourt, Brace & World, 1962), which was influenced somewhat by transfor-mational-generative grammar; further developed in *English Syn-tax: A Book of Programmed Lesson; An Introduction to Transfor-mational Grammar* (New York: Harcourt, Brace and World, 1964).

[52] H. A. Gleason, *An Introduction to Descriptive Linguis-tics* (New York: Holt, Rinehart & Winston, 1961); *Linguistics and English Grammar* (New York: Holt, Rinehart & Winston, 1965), which contains several chapters of historical background, tra-cing the rise and development of descriptive linguistics and English grammar, and a rather extensive use of early transfor-mational-generative grammar.

[53] Robert Funk, *A Beginning-Intermediate Grammar of Helle-istic Greek* (Missoula, MT: SBL, 1973). Less significant is the pedagogical grammar of Eugene Van Ness Goetchius, *The Lan-guage of the New Testament* (New York: Scribners, 1965), who par-ticularly followed Fries, in contrast to Funk's use of Gleason, though Funk followed Gleason only in part.

[54] Funk, xxiv.

[55] Ibid., xxviii.

[56] Ibid., 14-15, 20.

[57] John Searle, "Chomsky's Revolution in Linguistics," in *n Noam Chomsky: Critical Essays*, ed. Gilbert Harman (Garden ity, N.Y.: Anchor, 1974) 3.

[1]For a realistic appraisal see John Searle, "Chomsky's
Revolution in Linguistics."

[2]Noam Chomsky, *Syntactic Structures* (The Hague: Mouton,
1957), hereafter *Structures*, a classroom version of parts of a
much longer work, "The Logical Structure of Linguistic Theory,"
MIT Library, 1955, (Mimeographed), which was not published until
recently, various chapters of it having been revised, as *The
Logical Structure of Linguistic Theory* (New York: Plenum, 1975),
hereafter *Logical Structure*, with an Introduction, written in
1973, which gives Chomsky's own historical account of the development of his linguistic theory.

[3]The implications were just as important for philosophy
and psychology. For a discussion of these matters see Justin
Leiber, *Noam Chomsky: A Philosophical Overview* (Boston: G. K.
Hall, 1975), who carefully reveiws the background issues and
the progression of Chomsky's own philosophical thought.

[4]Noam Chomsky, "Morphophonemics of Modern Hebrew" (M.A.
thesis, University of Pennsylvania, 1951); "Transformation Analysis" (Ph.D. dissertation, University of Pennsylvania, 1955).
The latter became part of the longer work mentioned in n. 2.

[5]Zellig Harris, *Methods in Structural Linguistics* (Chicago: University of Chicago, 1951) 1. The preface is dated 1947.
The paperback edition appeared in 1960 (also University of Chicago) with the shortened title *Structural Linguistics*, "methods"
being out of vogue after 1957.

[6]Ibid., 262.

[7]Ibid., 271-72.

[8]Ibid., 279; for "noun phrase" and "verb phrase" see 287,
291, 331. This example is given in anticipation of the generative model which will follow. Harris' major symbols are: T =
Determiner, D = Adverb, A = Adjective, N = Noun, V = Verb, P =
Preposition.

[9]Ibid., 363.

[10]Ibid., 367-75.

[11]We have presented Harris' *Methods* in this much detail
because it was the basis for Chomsky's original work in linguistics. In fact, as a student, he proofread Harris' *Methods* (Harris, *Methods*, v; Chomsky, *Logical Structures*, 25, where Chomsky

begins the autobiographical sketch that includes his own evaluation of Harris' approach).

[12] Zellig Harris, "Discourse Analysis," *Language* 28 (1952)
1-30, reprinted in *The Structure of Language: Readings in the
Philosophy of Language*, eds. Jerry Fodor and Jerrold J. Katz
(Englewood Cliffs, N.J.: Prentice-Hall, 1964) 355-83.

[13] Ibid., 355.

[14] Ibid., 371.

[15] Ibid., 373.

[16] Ibid., 372.

[17] Zellig Harris, "Co-occurrence and Transformation in Linguistic Structure," *Language* 33 (1957) 283-340, also reprinted
in Fodor and Katz, *The Structure of Language*, 155-210.

[18] Ibid., 162.

[19] Ibid., 167.

[20] This comparison is made by Dell Hymes, in "Review of
Noam Chomsky," *Language* 48 (1972) 416-27; reprinted in Harman,
On Noam Chomsky, 316-32.

[21] Chomsky, *Structures*, 11.

[22] Noam Chomsky, *Current Issues in Linguistic Theory* (The
Hague: Mouton, 1964) 9; hereafter *Issues*.

[23] *Structures*, 13.

[24] See the discussion of "Simplicity and the Form of Grammars," *Logical Structure*, 113-28, and the clarification in Noam
Chomsky, *Aspects of the Theory of Syntax* (Cambridge: MIT, 1965),
hereafter *Aspects*, 37-38.

[25] *Structures*, 49-56.

[26] *Issues*, 28-30. For further discussion, see *Aspects*, 30-
37.

[27] Noam Chomsky, *Topics in the Theory of Generative Grammar*
(The Hague: Mouton, 1966), hereafter *Topics*, 22.

[28] Here we follow Chomsky, *Aspects*, 27-30.

[29] See Noam Chomsky, *Language and Mind* (New York: Harcourt
Brace Jovanovich, 1968, enlarged edition 1972), and more recently, *Reflections on Language* (New York: Pantheon Books, 1975).

[30] *Aspects*, 27.

[31] *Aspects*, 30-34. The relationship between linguistic theory and language acquisition is stated explicitly by Chomsky in
Logical Structure, 9-13. For a popular survey of the study of

language acquisition see Breyne Moskowitz, "The Acquisition of Language," *Scientific American* 239 (November, 1978) 92ff.

[32] Leiber, *Noam Chomsky*, 54.

[33] Chomsky's popular writings deal only very summarily with his treatment of linguistic models, e.g., *Structures*, 18-33; *Aspects*, 13-15; *Issues*, 111-13. The detailed argumentation is in technical articles: the most basic is "Three Models for the Description of Language," hereafter "Three Models," *I. R. E. Transactions on Information Theory*, Vol. IT-2 (1956) 113-24, reprinted in *Readings in Mathematical Psychology* II, eds. R. Duncan Luce, Robert B. Bush and Eugene Galenter (New York: Wiley, 1956); various aspects of theoretical models are discussed in three articles in *Handbook of Mathematical Psychology* II, eds. Luce, Bush and Galenter (New York: Wiley, 1963), viz., two by Chomsky and George A. Miller, "Introduction to the Formal Analysis of Natural Languages," 269-321, and "Finitary Models of Language Users," 419-91; one by Chomsky, "Formal Properties of Grammars," 323-418. All three articles have bibliographies referring to even more technical literature. A more popularized exposition is Noam Chomsky, "Explanatory Models in Linguistics" in *Logic, Methodology and Philosophy of Science*, eds. Ernest Nagel, Patrick Suppes and Alfred Tarski (Stanford: Stanford University, 1962) 528-50. That same volume contains two brief summaries which focus on models: Y. Bar-Hillel, "Some Recent Results in Theoretical Linguistics," 551-557, and Yuen RenChao, "Models in Linguistics and Models in General," 558-66.

[34] Leiber, *Noam Chomsky*, 67; see entire section, 54-71.

[35] See especially his "Formal Properties of Grammars" (n. 33).

[36] See the brief historical mention in Bar-Hillel, "Some Recent Results...," 552, and Leiber, *Noam Chomsky*, 78; though in *Logical Structures*, 40, Chomsky disclaims having had any serious interest in the matter.

[37] E.g., Charles Hockett, *A Manual of Phonology* (Baltimore: Waverly, 1955), suggested by Chomsky, *Structures*, 20.

[38] Chomsky, "Three Models," 114-16. In "Formal Properties of Grammars" he outlines ways in which a digital computer can be more "powerful," i.e., giving it more complex sets of instructions. However, to achieve even observational adequacy would involve processes which have not been proven possible for a finite state device.

[39] Chomsky and Miller, "Finitary Models of Language Users," 470.

[40] Chomsky, "Formal Properties of Grammars," 390.

[41] *Structures*, 18.

[42] Ibid., 26.

[43] Ibid., 111. The notational symbols are those given in

Appendix I, except for Determiner, which is here "T."

[44] Adapted from Howard Maclay, "Overview" to the section on Linguistics in *Semantics: An Interdisciplinary Reader in Philosophy, Linguistics and Psychology*, eds. Danny Steinberg and Leon Jakobovits (Cambridge: Cambridge University, 1971) 166.

[45] See above, p. 16.

[46] *Structures*, 34-48; *Issues*, 34-50; also "Three Models," 120-123.

[47] The asterisk * is used in front of a string to indicate that it is grammatically unacceptable.

[48] *Structures*, 44.

[49] Maclay, "Overview," 166.

[50] Chomsky, *Issues*, 13.

[51] For his sample list see Harris, "Discourse Analysis," 375-76.

[52] *Topics*, 51-2 for terminology; a brief account is found in *Structures*, 61-84; a more detailed discussion is presented by Noam Chomsky, "A Transformational Approach to Syntax," in *Proceedings of the Third Texas Conference on Problems of Linguistic Analysis in English, 1958*, ed. Archibald A. Hill (Austin, Texas: University of Texas, 1962), reprinted in Fodor and Katz, *The Structure of Language*, 211-45, from which references are taken.

[53] Chomsky, "A Transformational Approach to Syntax," 223.

[54] This is formulated in terms of Chomsky's theory in *Structures*, but is seen more clearly in his "A Transformational Approach to Syntax," 229-30. The actual example is on page 237. The details of the transformations for (12) and (13) are more involved and will not be presented here. They are summarized in Chomsky and Miller, "Finitary Models of Language Users," 476-80.

[55] For other discussion of issues debated after *Structures* see *Current Issues in Linguistic Theory*; *Topics in the Theory of Generative Grammar*; and *Language and Mind*, Ch. 2.

[56] For his description see Chomsky, *Aspects*, 79-111, 164-92.

[57] Morris Halle and Noam Chomsky, *The Sound Pattern of English* (New York: Harper & Row, 1968).

[58] See John Lyons, "Generative Syntax," in *New Horizons in Linguistics*, ed. John Lyons (Baltimore: Penguin, 1970) 125; Lyons, *Noam Chomsky*, 87; John Searle, "Chomsky's Revolution in Linguistics," 14.

[59] Chomsky, *Aspects*, 15-17.

[60] But contrary to Chomsky, *Aspects*, 103-5, 132, the passive transformation apparently cannot be tied to a deep structure marker, but must rather be left as an optional stylistic transformation.

[61] In addition to *Aspects*, a more succinct presentation of the sequential application of T rules is found in Chomsky, *Topics*, 59-66.

[62] In Noam Chomsky, *Studies on Semantics in Generative Grammar* (The Hague: Mouton, 1972), 62-119, hereafter *Semantics*, a collection of three articles, defending and partly expanding the theory of *Aspects*. "Deep Structure, Surface Structure and Semantic Interpretation" was written in 1968 (see bibliography, *Semantics*, 200), and included lecture material from 1966 (*Semantics*, 88, n. 20).

[63] Ibid., 75.

[64] Chiefly McCawley, Lakoff and Fillmore, whose various articles are listed in the bibliography supplied with the article in *Semantics*, 118-119.

[65] Ibid., 69.

[66] Ibid., 88. This is the portion from the earlier lectures.

[67] Ibid., 107, 108. [This probably has more to do with the inherent features of "shall" and "will," as Bishop John Wallis observed long ago in his *Grammatica Linguae Anglicanae* (1660); now in a new edition with translation and commentary by J. A. Kemp, *Grammar of the English Language* (New York: Longman, 1972) 338-39. See also Julian Boyd and J. P. Thorne, "The Semantics of Modal Verbs," *Journal of Linguistics* 5 (1969) 59-74, especially the discussion of "will" and "shall" on pages 62-65.]

[68] Ibid., 113.

[69] Noam Chomsky, "Some Empirical Issues in the Theory of Transformational Grammar," also in *Semantics*, 120-202 (again with a bibliography of all the papers and dissertations he responds to), where Chomsky again argues that many of the differences are more notational than substantial.

[70] Ibid., 180, 197.

[71] The frequently used example is: in EST the word "kill" is inserted into a basic string by a lexical transformation for a terminal item labeled V (with the proper feature markings such as transitive), whereas "generative semantics" wants the base phrase-structure to indicate "cause to be not alive," which EST considers the function of the lexicon and not the phrase-marker. For an exposition see George Lakoff's dissertation, *Irregularity in Syntax* (New York: Holt, Rinehart & Winston, 1970) 100. The most direct statement of the contrast is contained in Jerrold J. Katz, "Interpretive Semantics Vs. Generative Semantics," *Foundations of Language* 6 (1970) 220-59. A diagram contrasting the two is on 230-231 and Lakoff's example is treated on 244-

45, 251-53. Katz condenses the issue thus:
> The major difference . . . between the theory that sub-
> scribes to the hypothesis that there exists a level of
> deep syntactic structure and the theory that does not
> is that the former claims that the best choice of ob-
> jects with which to begin the transformational process
> of generating representations of surface structure is
> also the best choice of objects with which to start in
> the process of generating semantic interpretations,
> namely, phrase-markers representing deep syntactic
> structure, whereas the latter claims that the best
> choice of objects with which to begin the transforma-
> tional process of generating representations of sur-
> face structure is semantic interpretations themselves.
> Accordingly, these theories assign the role of being
> the primary link in the connecting of sound and mean-
> ing in natural languages to different aspects of syn-
> tactic structure. Generative semantics assigns this
> role to the syntactic relations expressed by the lex-
> icon and transformational components, whereas interpre-
> tive semantics assigns this role to the syntactic rela-
> tions expressed by the rules of the base subcomponent
> of the syntactic component (257).

Katz supports this by arguing that "semantic representations
are linguistic universals" and "phonetic representations and
surface phrase markers are highly language specific" (258), and
it is the deep syntactic structure that "embodies the complex
network of connections between the language universal and the
language particular syntactic structures that must underlie
the systematic correlation of sound and meaning" (259).

The fullest description of interpretive semantics is contained in Ray Jackendoff, *Semantic Interpretation in Generative
Grammar* (Cambridge: MIT, 1972). Another Chomsky student active-
ly defending EST is Adrian Akmajian ("Aspects of the Grammar of
Focus in English" [Ph.D. dissertation, MIT, 1970]).

The subsequent discussion on this issue has dealt with various combinations of the deep, surface and "shallow" levels of
structure which are involved in the semantic interpretation of
a sentence.

[72] Noam Chomsky, "Remarks on Nominalization," the other article
in *Semantics* (11-61, written in 1967 [*Semantics*, 200], which
previously appeared in *Readings in English Transformational
Grammar*, eds. Roderick A. Jacobs and Peter S. Rosenbaum [Waltham,
MA: Ginn & Co., 1970] 184-221) 17.

[73] Robert B. Lees, *The Grammar of English Nominalizations* (The
Hague: Mouton, 1960).

[74] Ibid., vi.

[75] See above, p. 19.

[76] Lees, *The Grammar of English Nominalizations*, xvii.

[77] E.g., 1) "factive nominal," i.e., *That* and *WH*- (who, what,
where, why, when) clauses which, respectively, make an assertion
(*That he came* was obvious), or answer a question (*What he did*
was obvious); 2) "action nominal," i.e., *-ing* (his strong

objecting . . .) and derived verbal (His strong objection . . .)
constructions; 3) "agentive nominal," i.e., *-er* forms (buyer,
seller); 4) "gerundive nominal," a more precise formulation of
the *-ing* in 2); 5) "infinitival nominal," phrases with *to* used
in various ways; 6) "abstractive nominal," e.g., *-ness*, *-tion*.
He also dealt with some adjectival transformations which do not
concern us here. His second main area of investigation covered
"nominal compounds," which he analyzed as derived from various
sentence-types. His model nominal compounds include *girlfriend*,
doctor's office, *talking machine*, *assembly plant* and *steamboat*.
(They certainly are not limited to two words; later discussion
enjoyed using *jet engine replacement parts depot*.)

[78] *Issues*, 47.

[79] *Aspects*, 184.

[80] Ibid., 186.

[81] Ibid., 219-220.

[82] See n. 72, hereafter "Remarks."

[83] "Remarks," 17.

[84] Ibid., 22.

[85] Ibid., 30.

[86] Ibid., 60.

[87] Thomas Wasow and Thomas Roeper, "On the Subject of Gerunds,"
Foundations of Language 8 (1972) 44-61.

[88] Ibid., 45-6, where two sets of examples are given also.

[89] Ibid., 58.

[90] Joan Bresnan, "Theory of Complementation in English Syntax"
(Ph.D. dissertation, MIT, 1972). See Joan Bresnan, "On Comple-
mentizers: Towards a Syntactic Theory of Complement Types,"
Foundations of Language 6 (1970) 297-321.

[91] The best initial discussion is found in Noam Chomsky, "Conditions on Transformations," in *Festschrift for Morris Halle*,
eds. Stephen Anderson and Paul Kiparsky (New York: Holt, Rinehart and Winston, 1973) 232-86; reprinted in Noam Chomsky, *Essays on Form and Interpretation* (New York: Elsevier North-Holland,
1977) 81-160. The same approach is more fully developed in Noam
Chomsky and Howard Lasnik, "Filters and Control," *Linguistic Inquiry* 8 (1977) 425-504. Chomsky's "On WH-Movement," in *Formal
Syntax*, eds. Peter W. Culicover, Thomas Wasow and Adrian Akmajian (New York: Academic, 1977) 71-132, assumes this theory of
COMP while addressing other issues.

[92] "Filters and Control," 444.

[93] Though originally this was meant to apply to every S, we
will adopt it only for embeds.

[94] "Filters and Control," 456.

[95] "Conditions on Transformations," 237; "Filters and Control," 439.

[96] Joseph Emonds, "Root and Structure-Preserving Transforma- tions" (Ph.D. dissertation, MIT, 1970); now published as *A Trans- formational Approach to English Syntax* (New York: Academic, 1976). The importance of this work for Chomsky can be seen in Noam Chomsky, *Reflections on Language* (New York: Random House, 1975), ch. 3 and in "Filters and Control."

[97] In addition to the references cited in n. 91 and n. 96, the balance of *Essays on Form and Interpretation*, especially his summarizing Introduction and "Conditions on Rules of Grammar," 163-210, reprinted from *Linguistic Analysis* 2 (1976); and lecture four in the forthcoming *Rules and Representations*, the 1979 Kant Lectures delivered at Stanford University, Palo Alto, CA, Janu- ary 1979.

[98] "Conditions on Rules," 205; "On WH- Movement," 72.

[99] Emmon Bach, "Comments on the Paper of Chomsky," in *Formal Syntax*, 133-55.

[100] E.g., David Lightfoot, "On Traces and Conditions on Rules," in *Formal Syntax*, 207-38.

[1]For a sample see the current issues of any of the linguistic journals cited in the previous chapter.

[2]The first place where one might expect evidence of such work to appear is in the papers presented at the annual meeting of the Society of Biblical Literature, especially to its Linguistic Group. However, those papers and discussions that incorporate a specific linguistics are almost invariably interested in some kind of structural or discourse analysis of biblical texts. Only at the most recent meeting (November 1978) was there any indication by several participants of an awareness of the challenge of TG grammar to the dominant structuralist mode.

[3]Sponsored by the Center for Hermeneutical Studies in Hellenistic and Modern Culture at the Graduate Theological Union in Berkeley, CA. Edward C. Hobbs is director of the project, for which Irene Lawrence and Daryl Schmidt have been Research Fellows.

[4]By Edward C. Hobbs with Irene Lawrence and Daryl Schmidt (Berkeley: GTU, 1977, revised 1978), hereafter *Outline Grammar*.

[5]For the most part these follow the conventional rules of TG grammars, i.e., they would be close to the PS rules for Universal Grammar. The primary departure from current TG grammar is in the treatment of NP within VP by rules (1d) and (1e), which reflects the linguistic theory developed by Edward Hobbs in the *Outline Grammar* (p. 2.61) that *every* NP in VP is an adverbial part of a surface-level transformational cycle that assigns a morphological feature to the adverbial function of the NP. E.g., the accusative NP ("the direct object") is characteristically an adverbial of limit/extent. Likewise, prepositions are treated as preposed ("Chomsky-adjoined") adverbial-markers, also part of the same cycle.

[6]See above, p. 24.

[7]For a good discussion and summary of the various arguments and issues involved in subcategorizing verbs see chapter 9 in Adrian Akmajian and Frank Heny, *An Introduction to the Principles of Transformational Syntax* (Cambridge: MIT, 1975), hereafter Akmajian and Heny.

[8]For Chomsky's formalization see "The Structure of the Lexicon" in Chomsky, *Aspects*, 164-92, especially 164-70.

[9]Lists of such verbs can be found in Robertson, 1034-36, and Blass-Debrunner, 204-5.

¹⁰Henry G. Liddell and Robert Scott, eds., *A Greek-English Lexicon*, revised by Henry S. Jones and Roderick McKenzie (Oxford Clarendon, 1968), hereafter Liddell-Scott, 385.

¹¹See above, pp. 36-37.

¹²See Herbert W. Smyth, *Greek Grammar*, revised by Gordon M. Messing (Cambridge: Harvard University, 1920, 1956), hereafter Smyth-Messing, 245; Moulton-Howard, 394. The label "Factitive" is not to be confused with the "factive" presupposition discuss in Paul Kiparsky and Carol Kiparsky, "Fact," in *Progress in Linguistics*, eds. Manfred Bierwisch and Karl E. Heidolph (The Hague Mouton, 1970) 143-173.

¹³In order to express these relationships more explicitly we present the following set of PS diagrams as a working hypothesis, given here only in outline with the details left for further investigation. For the deep structure (initial PM) for (5c), we suggest (5c<u>i</u>):

(5)   (c)<u>i</u>   ἐδηλώθη . . . ὅτι

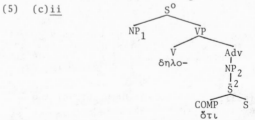

S̄¹ by itself corresponds to (5b): ὅτι . . . δῆλον. S̄¹ can also be embedded into a VP whose primary feature marker is +FACTITIVE which can have two transformations: 1) insert a lexical verb that has the +FACTITIVE feature--in Greek, ποιέω (see Mt 26:73), or 2) insert a lexical form of the embedded VP which has that feature--in Greek, δηλόω, resulting in a structure like (5c<u>ii</u>):

(5)   (c)<u>ii</u>

In the transformational process several nodes (S̄¹ and NP₃ have been deleted. This operation has been established on other grounds as part of the TG linguistic theory. (See John Robert Ross, "A Proposed Rule of Tree-Pruning," in *Modern Studies in English*, eds. David A. Reibel and Sanford A Schane [Englewood

Cliffs, N.J.: Prentice-Hall, 1969].) When T_{PASS} is applied to
(5c<u>ii</u>) the result is (5c<u>iii</u>):

(5) (c)<u>iii</u>

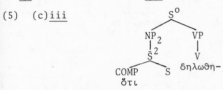

i.e., $\bar{S}^2$ (the original ὅτι-embed) is again functioning as the
subject of a VP, similar to (5c), which is passive, similar to
(3b), whose stem is δηλ-, similar to (5b) and to the original
$\bar{S}^1$.

[14]The rule of grammar involved is: the more determined
of the two nominative NPs is the dominant NP (functioning as
subject), but that is still not self-evident here.

[15]See the discussion in Akmajian and Heny, chapter 9, especially the diagrams on p. 336, which involve the syntax of our
"cognition" verb class.

[16]Thus

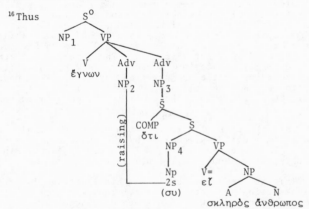

[17]Many of the instances of this construction are subject
to scribal alteration, though not the following: Jn 3:21; 8:54;
9:8; Ac 4:13; 1 Cor 3:20; 14:37; 16:15; Gal 1:11; 1 Th 2:1;
2 Th 2:4.

[18]See C. H. Turner, "Marcan Usage," *Journal of Theological
Studies* 28 (1927) 9-15.

[19]We have not cited any versions because in principle each
language has its own embedding devices, so lack of a word explicitly corresponding to ὅτι is not direct evidence that ὅτι
was lacking in the manuscript being translated; thus the trans-
lator may simply have been using a different embedding transformation, either by choice or by limitation of the language.

[20] In light of the discussion below on deleting ὅτι with Commands, and since the repeated statement here is also a Command, we would suggest that the reading without ὅτι is in fact the correct reading and therefore this example should not be part of the list, for the same reason that Jn 5:11, 12 are not. This further indicates the general overall accuracy of P[75] in contrast to P[66].

[21] The other apparent exception is Jn 9:17 ὁ δὲ εἶπεν ὅτι προφήτης ἐστίν, where ὅτι is persistently interpreted as introducing direct discourse. However, since John never uses it elsewhere in that way, some other explanation must be sought. It should be seen in the context of giving an answer to the preceding question: τί σὺ λέγεις περὶ αὐτοῦ, ὅτι ἠνέῳξέν σου τοὺς ὀφθαλμούς; This ὅτι is usually taken as an awkward causal with the sense "with regard to the fact that." (See Rudolf Bultmann *The Gospel of John: A Commentary* [Philadelphia: Westminster, 1971] 334, which refers to a special Hebraic use cited in Blass Debrunner; and C. K. Barrett, *The Gospel According to John* [London: SPCK, 1960] 298, which refers to a special category in Lidell-Scott for certain passages in Plato!) Our analysis of the stylistic use of ὅτι in Johannine discourse suggests that the more likely syntax of 9:17 is as follows: τί λέγεις ὅτι S = "Why do you say S," where S is the response the formerly blind man had given to the earlier question πῶς ("How?"), viz., he explains the actual process of *how* Jesus made mud, etc. After repeating this twice (9:10-11 and 9:15), the question is clarified, πῶς δύναται ("How is it possible?") and then rephrased, τί λέγεις ὅτι S ("Why do you keep saying S?") with ὅτι functioning to embed indirect discourse. The answer (ὁ δὲ εἶπεν) is then ὅτι προφήτης ἐστίν ("Because he is a prophet."), and not the embedding device of quotation marks, as it is usually assumed to be. We see this same use of ὅτι in answer to τί in Mt 13:11, Lk 15:27; 19:34, though it is seldom ever so translated.

[22] This is not really in the form of the original statement but is itself modelled afted 1:30 by the redactor. See Raymond E. Brown, *The Gospel According to John* vol. I (Anchor Bible; Garden City, N.Y.: Doubleday, 1968) 35.

[23] This is the only example on this list that is part of a narrative section and not discourse. Thus many scribes thought that ὅτι was necessary with the repeated discourse.

[24] See n. 19.

[25] Blass-Debrunner, 247.

[26] See Bernard P. Grenfell and Arthur S. Hunt, eds., *The Oxyrhynchus Papyri* vol. XIV (London: Egypt Exploration Society, 1920) 144:
    ὥπου ἡπάντηκά σου . . . καὶ εἴρηκα σου ὥτι δὸς ἐμοὶ κέρμα
    . . . , καὶ εἶπές με ὥτι . . . .

    When I met you . . . and said to you, "Give me some money
    . . . ," and you said to me, ". . . ."

[27]Compare lines 8-9:

γιγνώσκιν σε θέλω, κυρία μου ἀδελφή, ἄπελθε . . . .
I want you to know, my dear sister, Go . . . .

and line 13:

οἶδες καὶ σὺ ὅτι οὐδὲν ἔχωμεν . . . .
You too know that we have no . . . .

[28]Curiously, all three editions of *The Greek New Testament* of the United Bible Societies do omit ὅτι at Mk 4:21, but include it at 8:4.

[29]See our discussion above on the Johannine material.

[30]Blass-Debrunner, 247. The error is in the German also--it is not a typographical error in the English translation.

[31]See Frederic G. Kenyon, *The Chester Beatty Biblical Papyri. Fasciculus III Supplement. Pauline Epistles. Plates.* (London: Emery Walker, 1937) folio 14 verso.

[32]For lists of such verbs in the New Testament see Moulton-Turner, 103-4, and Blass-Debrunner, 199-200; for the papyri, see Robert C. Horn, *The Use of the Subjunctive and Optative Moods in the Non-Literary Papyri* (Philadelphia: University of Pennsylvania, 1926) 103-116.

[33]See the suggested "Auxiliary Features" of Modal, Aspect and Time in Hobbs, *Outline Grammar*, 4.01, which are to be distinguished from "auxiliary verbs." The auxiliary feature "Modal" is a gradient marked from weak to strong along a scale of VOLITION/POSSIBILITY. The feature marking is then transformed into either a morphological marking or into a chaining verb (sometimes called "catenative" and traditionally "auxiliary verb"). E.g., the weak VOLITION marking *Wish* is transformed into either an optative form of the matrix verb or into a chaining verb--θέλω/βούλομαι--with the infinitive form of the matrix verb. *Command* is the strongest VOLITION marking and is transformed into subjunctive and imperative forms.

[34]The entire matter of the AUX node is only now beginning to receive widespread linguistic attention, so there is still much flux in the terminlogy used. For a discussion of modality using binary gradients corresponding to VOLITION and POSSIBILITY see Geoffrey Leech, *Towards a Semantic Description of English* (London: Longman's, 1969) 203-5; Randolph Quirk, Sidney Greenbaum, Geoffrey Leech and Jan Svartrik, *A Grammar of Contemporary English* (New York: Seminar Press, 1972) 97-102. A somewhat different notational system is used for analyzing essentially the same modal markings in Julian Boyd and J. P. Thorne, "The Semantics of Modal Verbs." However, they confine "modal" to the mark of the "illocutionary potential of the sentence," which is roughly equivalent to VOLITION (on the part of the speaker), by distinguishing it both from the feature marking +NECESSITY and from the marks of sentences whose only illocutionary potential is "statement," which together roughly correspond to POSSIBILITY. For a quite different analysis of the "pragmatics" of modality

see Asa Kasher, "Mood Implicatures: A Logical Way of Doing Ge
erative Pragmatics," *Theoretical Linguistics* 1 (1974) 6-38.

[35] Also fading from regular use was ὡς as COMP for declar
ative embeds in "cognition" phrases, while πῶς was just beginning on the course that led it to become the main COMP of Mode
Greek (as πῶς). For a discussion of these see A. N. Jannaris,
"Misreadings and Misrenderings in the New Testament. III," *Th*
Expositor V (1899) 142-53; Moulton-Turner, 137; Blass-Debrunne
203.

[36] See the discussion of the question transformation in
Hobbs, *Outline Grammar*, 5.21-22, 5.31.

[37] See above, pp. 47-8.

[38] See above, pp. 49-50.

[39] Recent literature generally contrasts these as "non-
modals" and "modals," because the latter are transformed into
"modal verbs" in English. However, if we want to talk about t
modality of each sentence apart from its morphology, we lack
appropriate labels. We have chosen to use a suggestion that
originated in Julian Boyd's seminar on AUX (Fall, 1978, Univer
sity of California, Berkeley, in discussion between Boyd and
Hobbs) that "índicative" be used as the label for the "non-
modal" modals (with the accent to distinguish it from the "indicative mood" as a morphological label).

[40] Traditional grammars see this as Hellenistic confusion
See Moulton-Turner, 49: "Confusion of relative and interrogative pronouns is usual in Hellenistic Greek."

[41] The vowel is usually *omicron*, as in ὅς, ὅτι and ὅπως,
though lengthened to *omega* in ὥστε. The origin of the ἵνα for
is unknown, and since there are no other ἵ-forms anywhere in the
COMP category, it is likely that it originated by analogy to t
ὅ-forms. See Karl Brugmann, *Griechische Grammatik*, 285.

[42] Chomsky formulates this as ±WH. See above, p. 38.

[43] "The interrogative use of εἰ is derived from the conditional meaning *if*," Smyth-Messing, 602 (§2671.b).

[44] Jannaris suggests that this use of εἰ in the New Testa-
ment is really a scribal misreading of ἤ, which is other times
misread as ἤ. See A. N. Jannaris, *An Historical Greek Grammar*
(London: Macmillan, 1897) 478. If Jannaris is correct the like
New Testament examples are Mt 12:10; 19:3; 20:15; Mk 8:23;
Lk 13:23; 22:49; Ac 1:6; 7:1; 19:2; 21:37; 22:25; 23:9.

[45] Smyth-Messing, 604, gives one example of each from Aes-
chines (1.84; 2.36) and there is a papyrus example (3rd century
B.C.) in Edwin Mayser, *Grammatik der Griechischen Papyri aus de*
Ptolemäerzeit II.3 (Berlin: Gruyter, 1934) 53:

P Hal 8.6 προσάγαγε αὐτόν, ὅπως ἐπισκέψωμαι καὶ αὐτός, εἰ μὴ
δύναται τὴν χρείαν παρέχεσθαι (232a)

Bring him in so that I myself may observe whether
he is not able to render service

[46]Lists of such verbs are found in Moulton-Turner, 137-8,
nd in Blass-Debrunner, 204.

[47]It is characteristic of the traditional discussions of
"style" that Luke's preference for infinitive constructions is
ot even mentioned in the chapter on "The Style of Luke-Acts"
n Moulton-Turner, *Style*, 45-63, nor in the section on "The Lan-
uage and Style of Acts" in Ernst Haenchen, *The Acts of the
postles: A Commentary* (Philadelphia: Westminster, 1971) 72-
1.

[48]On the parallel use of ἵνα and Inf, see Ernest De Witt
urton, *Syntax of the Moods and Tenses in New Testament Greek*
Chicago: University of Chicago, 1900; reprinted, Grand Rapids:
regel, 1976) 87-92.

[49]For a thorough discussion of semantics in a TG framework,
ee Jerrold J. Katz, *Semantic Theory* (New York: Harper & Row,
972).

[50]Such use is common in the papyri. See J. H. Moulton and
. Milligan, *Vocabulary*, 598.

NOTES - SUMMARY AND CONCLUSION

[1]For an initial application of this to one particular New
estament problem, see Daryl Schmidt, "Pauline Syntax: The Trans-
ormational Patterns of 1-2 Thess," paper read at a meeting of
he Society of Biblical Literature, New Orleans, LA, November
978.

CATEGORY SYMBOLS AND INSTRUCTION SYMBOLS*

A	adjective or adnominal
AP	adjective phrase
Adv	adverb or adverbial
<Ap>	appositive
Asp	aspect marking (node of AUX)
AUX	auxiliary (node of S)
COMP	complementizer
D	determiner:
Da	article
Dd	demonstrative
De	emphatic
Dn	nominal
Dq	quantifier
M	modal marking (node of AUX)
N	noun or nominal
N^n	noun in nominative case
N^q	noun in an oblique case:
N^a	noun in accusative case
N^d	noun in dative case
N^g	noun in genitive case
N^v	noun in vocative case
NP	noun phrase
NP^x	noun phrase in various cases
Np	pronoun
NEG	marker for negative
NOM	nominalization
[P]	reserved for "phrase," as in "noun phrase," etc.
PASS	marker for passive
Pr	preposition
PP	prepositional phrase
Q	marker for "question"
REL	"relative" transformation
S	sentence

$\bar{S}$	embedded sentence
S^1, S^2,...	embedded sentences within a matrix sentence (S^0)
T	transformation
T_{XXX}	specific transformation (e.g., T_{NOM})
Tm	time marking (node of AUX)
V	verb
V=	equative verb
Vif	infinitive verb
Vpt	participle
Vnt	intransitive verb
Vtr	transitive verb
Vc	chaining verb
V=if	infinitive of equative verb (etc.)
V^{ps}	verb in passive voice
V^{md}	verb in middle voice
V^{sj}	verb in subjunctive mood
V^{op}	verb in optative mood
V^{mp}	verb in imperative mood
Vpt^{ps}	passive participle (etc.)
VC	verb chain
VP	verb phrase
VPif	infinitive verb phrase (etc.)
Π-	marker for Π- function (in PM^D)
Δ	"dummy" terminal symbol
Δ=	"dummy" equative
PM	phrase marker
PM^D	deep structure ("initial") phrase marker
PM^S	surface structure phrase marker
—>	"rewrite left symbol as right symbol(s)" [PS rule]
=>	"transform left string to right string" [T rule]
∅	null symbol ("delete")
≡	equivalence or identity
( )	optional items
{ }	items so enclosed form a set
/	items so separated are disjunctive (alternative members of the set), or indicates "in the environment of"

*Adapted from E. C. Hobbs, *An Outline of a Transformational-Generative Grammar of Hellenistic Greek*, page 0.11

SELECTED BIBLIOGRAPHY

I. Greek Language

land, Kurt, ed. *Synopsis Quattuor Evangeliorum*. 4th ed. Stuttgart: Württembergische Bibelanstalt, 1967.

land, Kurt; Black, Matthew; Metzger, Bruce M.; and Wikgren, Allen, eds. *The Greek New Testament*. New York: United Bible Societies, 1966, 1968, 1975.
The last two editions included Carlo M. Martini on the editorial committee and were in cooperation with the Institute for New Testament Textual Research, Münster/Westphalia.

arrett, C. K. *The Gospel According to John*. London: SPCK, 1960.

auer, Walter. *A Greek-English Lexicon of the New Testament and Other Early Christian Literature*. Translated by William F. Arndt and F. Wilbur Gingrich. Chicago: University of Chicago, 1957.

lass, Friedrich. *Grammatik des neutestamentlichen Griechisch*. Göttingen: Vandenhoeck & Ruprecht, 1896. Translated by Henry St. John Thackeray: *Grammar of New Testament Greek*. London: Macmillan, 1898.

lass, Friedrich and Debrunner, Albert. *Grammatik des neutestamentlichen Griechisch*. Edited by Friedrich Rehkopf. Göttingen: Vandenhoeck & Ruprecht, 1976.

lass, Friedrich and Debrunner, Albert. *A Greek Grammar of the New Testament and Other Early Christian Literature*. Translated by Robert W. Funk. Chicago: University of Chicago, 1961.

opp, Franz. *Ueber das Konjagationssystem der Sanskritsprache*. Frankfurt-am-Main, 1816.
Developed into *Vergleichende Grammatik*, 1833-1852.

rown, Raymond E. *The Gospel According to John*. 2 vols. Anchor Bible. Garden City, N.Y.: Doubleday, 1968.

rugmann, Karl. *Griechische Grammatik*. Handbuch der Klassischen Altertums-Wissenschaft II.1. 4th ed. Edited by Albert Thumb. Munich: Beck, 1913.

ultmann, Rudolf. *The Gospel of John: A Commentary*. Translated by G. R. Beasley-Murray, R. W. N. Hoare, and J. K. Riches. Philadelphia: Westminster, 1971.

Burton, Ernest De Witt. *Syntax of the Moods and Tenses in New Testament Greek.* Chicago: University of Chicago, 1900; reprint ed., Grand Rapids: Kregel, 1976.

Buttmann, Alexander. *A Grammar of New Testament Greek.* Translated by J. Henry Thayer. Andover: Warren Draper, 1873.

Deissmann, Adolf. *Light from the Ancient East.* Translated by L. R. M. Strachen. New York: George H. Doran, 1910; reprint ed., Grand Rapids: Baker, 1978.

Earle, Mortimer Lamson. "Some Remarks on the Moods of Will in Greek." In *The Classical Papers of Mortimer Lamson Earle* 219-22. New York: Columbia University, 1912.

Funk, Robert. *A Beginning-Intermediate Grammar of Hellenistic Greek.* Missoula, MT: Society of Biblical Literature, 19

Goetchius, Eugene Van Ness. *The Language of the New Testament.* New York: Scribners, 1965.

Goodwin, William Watson. *Syntax of the Moods and Tenses of the Greek Verb.* Boston: Ginn & Company, 1897.

Grenfell, Bernard P., and Hunt, Arthur S., eds. *The Oxyrhynchus Papyri.* Vol. XIV. London: Egypt Exploration Society, 19

Haenchen, Ernst. *The Acts of the Apostles: A Commentary.* Translated by Bernard Noble and Gerald Shinn. Philadelphia: Westminster, 1971.

Hatch, Edwin, and Redpath, Henry A. *A Concordance to the Septuagint.* 2 vols. Oxford: Clarendon, 1897; reprint ed., Graz, Austria: Akademische Druck- u. Verlagsanstalt, 1975

Hermann, Gottfried. *De emendanda ratione Graecae grammaticae.* Leipsig: Gerhard Fleischer, 1801.

Hobbs, Edward C., with Lawrence, Irene and Schmidt, Daryl. *An Outline of a Transformational-Generative Grammar of Hellenistic Greek.* Berkeley: Graduate Theological Union, 197 revised 1978. (Photocopied)

Horn, Robert C. *The Use of the Subjunctive and Optative Moods in the Non-Literary Papyri.* Philadelphia: University of Pennsylvania, 1926.

Jannaris, A. N. *An Historical Greek Grammar.* London: Macmill 1897.

_____. "Misreadings and Misrenderings in the New Testament Errors of Interpretation." *The Expositor* (1899) V.9, 29 310; V.10, 142-53.

Kenyon, Frederic G. *The Chester Beatty Biblical Papyri. Fasc culus III Supplement. Pauline Epistles. Plates.* Londo Emery Walker, 1937.

Liddell, Henry G., and Scott, Robert, eds. *A Greek-English Lexicon*. Revised by Henry S. Jones. With a Supplement edited by E. A. Barber. Oxford: Clarendon, 1968.

Mayser, Edwin. *Grammatik der Griechischen Papyri aus der Ptolemäerzeit*. 6 vols. Berlin: Gruyter, 1906-1934.

Metzger, Bruce M. *A Textual Commentary on the Greek New Testament*. New York: United Bible Societies, 1971.

Moulton, James H. *A Grammar of New Testament Greek*. 4 vols. Edinburgh: T. & T. Clark.
Vol. I: *Prolegomena*, by James H. Moulton, 1906. Vol. II: *Accidence and Word-Formation*, by James H. Moulton and Wilbert F. Howard, 1929. Vol. III: *Syntax*, by Nigel Turner, 1963. Vol. IV: *Style*, by Nigel Turner, 1976.

Moulton, James H., and Milligan, George. *The Vocabulary of the Greek Testament Illustrated from the Papyri and Other Non-Literary Sources*. Grand Rapids: Eerdmans, 1930, reprinted 1974.

Moulton, W. F., and Geden, A. S. *A Concordance to the Greek Testament*. Edinburgh: T. & T. Clark, 1897, reprinted 1970.

Nestle, Eberhard, ed. *Novum Testamentum Graece*. Revised by Kurt Aland and Erwin Nestle. Stuttgart: Württembergische Bibelanstalt, 1898-on; 25th ed., 1963.
The new (26th) edition will have the same Greek text as is in the UBS 3rd ed. and in the ninth edition of the *Synopsis Quattuor Evangeliorum*, also edited by Kurt Aland (United Bible Societies, 1976).

Rahlfs, Alfred, ed. *Septuaginta*. 2 vols. 8th ed. Stuttgart: Württembergische Bibelanstalt, 1935.

Robertson, A. T. *A Grammar of the Greek New Testament in the Light of Historical Research*. Nashville: Broadman, 1914, reprinted in 1934.

Rydbeck, Lars. "What Happened to New Testament Greek Grammar after Albert Debrunner?" *New Testament Studies* 21 (1975) 424-27.

Schmidt, Daryl. "Pauline Syntax: The Transformational Patterns of 1-2 Thess." Paper read at the meeting of the Society of Biblical Literature, New Orleans, LA, November 1978.

Smyth, Herbert W. *Greek Grammar*. Revised by Gordon M. Messing. Cambridge: Harvard University, 1920, 1956.

Thackeray, Henry St. John. *A Grammar of the Old Testament in Greek*. Cambridge: Cambridge University, 1909.

Turner, C. H. "Marcan Usage." *Journal of Theological Studies* 28 (1927) 9-30.

Winer, George B. *Grammatik des neutestamentlichen Sprachidioms*.
     Leipsig: Vogel, 1822.
          Seventh ed. enlarged by Gottlieb Lünnemann, 1867.
          Eighth ed. revised by Paul Schmiedel. Göttingen:
     Vandenhoeck & Ruprecht, 1894-98 (uncompleted).
          Sixth ed. (1866) translated by Edward Masson: *A Gram-
     mar of the New Testament Diction*. Edinburgh: T. & T.
     Clark, 1859. Revised by William F. Moulton: *A Treatise
     on the Grammar of New Testament Greek*. Edinburgh: T. &
     T. Clark, 1870.
          Seventh ed. (based on Masson) translated by J. Henry
     Thayer: *A Grammar of the Idiom of the New Testament*. An-
     dover: Warren Draper, 1869.
          English translations were also made of the first and
     fourth editions.

II. Linguistics

Akmajian, Adrian. "Aspects of the Grammar of Focus in English."
     Ph.D. dissertation, MIT, 1970.

Akmajian, Adrian, and Heny, Frank. *An Introduction to the Prin-
     ciples of Transformational Syntax*. Cambridge: MIT, 1975.

Anderson, Stephen, and Kiparsky, Paul, eds. *Festschrift for
     Morris Halle*. New York: Holt, Rinehart & Winston, 1973.

Bach, Emmon. "Comments on the Paper by Chomsky." In *Formal
     Syntax*, 133-55. Edited by Culicover, Wasow and Akmajian.

Bach, Emmon, and Harms, Robert T., eds. *Universals in Linguis-
     tic Theory*. New York: Holt, Rinehart & Winston, 1968.

Bar-Hillel, Y. "Some Recent Results in Theoretical Linguistics."
     In *Logic, Methodology and Philosophy of Science*, 551-57.
     Edited by Nagel, Suppes and Tarski.

Bierwisch, Manfred and Heidolph, Karl E. *Progress in Linguis-
     tics*. The Hague: Mouton, 1970.

Bloomfield, Leonard. *Language*. New York: Henry Holt, 1933.

Boas, Franz, ed. *Handbook of American Indian Languages*. Smith-
     sonian Institution: Bureau of American Ethnology, Bulle-
     tin 40. Washington: Govt. Printing Office, 1911-1938.

Boyd, Julian, and Thorne, J. P. "The Semantics of Modal Verbs."
     Journal of Linguistics 5 (1969) 59-74.

Bresnan, Joan. "On Complementizers: Towards a Syntactic Theory
     of Complement Types." *Foundations of Language* 6 (1970)
     297-321.

_____. "Theory of Complementation in English Syntax." Ph.D.
     dissertation, MIT, 1972.

Chomsky, Noam. *Aspects of the Theory of Syntax*. Cambridge,
     MIT, 1965.

Chomsky, Noam. *Cartesian Linguistics*. New York: Harper and
    Row, 1966.

_____. "Conditions on Rules of Grammar." In *Essays on Form
    and Interpretation*, 163-210.

_____. "Conditions on Transformations." In *Festschrift for
    Morris Halle*, 232-86. Edited by Anderson and Kiparsky.
    Reprinted in *Essays on Form and Interpretation*, 81-160.

_____. *Current Issues in Linguistic Theory*. The Hague: Mou-
    ton, 1964.

_____. "Deep Structure, Surface Structure and Semantic In-
    terpretation." In *Studies on Semantics*, 62-119.

_____. *Essays on Form and Interpretation*. New York: Else-
    vier North-Holland, 1977.

_____. "Explanatory Models in Linguistics." In *Logic, Meth-
    odology and Philosophy of Science*, 528-50. Edited by Na-
    gel, Suppes and Tarski.

_____. "Formal Properties of Grammars." In *Handbook of Math-
    ematical Psychology* II, 323-418. Edited by Luce, Bush,
    and Galenter.

_____. *Language and Mind*. New York: Harcourt, Brace and
    World, 1968; enlarged edition, 1972.

_____. *Language and Responsibility*. Based on conversations
    with Mitsou Ronat. Translated from the French by John
    Viertel. New York: Pantheon, 1979.

_____. *The Logical Structure of Linguistic Theory*. New York:
    Plenum, 1975.
        First appeared in 1955 (MIT Library, mimeographed).

_____. "On WH-Movement." In *Formal Syntax*, 71-132. Edited
    by Culicover, Wasow, and Akmajian.

_____. *Reflections on Language*. New York: Random House/Pan-
    theon Books, 1975.

_____. "Remarks on Nominalization." In *Studies on Semantics*,
    11-61.

_____. *Rules and Representations*. Forthcoming.
        The 1979 Kant Lectures. Stanford University, January
    1979.

_____. "Some Empirical Issues in the Theory of Transforma-
    tional Grammar." In *Studies on Semantics*, 120-202.

_____. *Studies on Semantics in Generative Grammar*. The
    Hague: Mouton, 1972.

_____. *Syntactic Structures*. The Hague: Mouton, 1957.

Chomsky, Noam. "Three Models for the Description of Language." *I. R. E. Transactions on Information Theory*, Vol. IT-2 (1956) 113-24. Reprinted in *Readings in Mathematical Psychology* II. Edited by Luce, Bush, and Galenter.

_____. *Topics in the Theory of Generative Grammar*. The Hague: Mouton, 1966.

_____. "A Transformational Approach to Syntax." In *The Structure of Language*, 211-45. Edited by Fodor and Katz.

Chomsky, Noam, and Lasnik, Howard. "Filters and Control." *Linguistic Inquiry* 8 (1977) 425-504.

Chomsky, Noam, and Miller, George A. "Finitary Properties of Grammars." In *Handbook of Mathematical Psychology* II, 419-91. Edited by Luce, Bush and Galenter.

Chomsky, Noam, and Miller, George A. "Introduction to the Formal Analysis of Natural Languages." In *Handbook of Mathematical Psychology* II, 269-321. Edited by Luce, Bush and Galenter.

Crystal, David. *Linguistics*. Baltimore: Penguin, 1971.

Culicover, Peter M.; Wasow, Thomas; and Akmajian, Adrian, eds. *Formal Syntax*. New York: Academic, 1977.

Emonds, Joseph. *A Transformational Approach to English Syntax*. New York: Academic, 1976.

Fillmore, Charles J., and Langendoen, D. Terence, eds. *Studies in Linguistic Semantics*. New York: Holt, Rinehart & Winston, 1971.

Fodor, Jerry, and Katz, Jerrold J., eds. *The Structure of Language: Readings in the Philosophy of Language*. Englewood Cliffs, N.J.: Prentice-Hall, 1964.

Fries, Charles C. *The Structure of English: An Introduction to the Construction of English Sentences*. New York: Harcourt, Brace, 1952.

Gleason, H. A. *An Introduction to Descriptive Linguistics and English Grammar*. New York: Holt, Rinehart & Winston, 1961.

_____. *Linguistics and English Grammar*. New York: Holt, Rinehart & Winston, 1965.

Halle, Morris, and Chomsky, Noam. *The Sound Pattern of English*. New York: Harper and Row, 1968.

Harman, Gilbert, ed. *On Noam Chomsky: Critical Essays*. Garden City, N.Y.: Anchor, 1974.

Harris, Zellig. "Co-occurrence and Transformation in Linguistic Structure." *Language* 33 (1957) 283-340. Reprinted in *The Structure of Language*, 155-210. Edited by Fodor and Katz.

Harris, Zellig. "Discourse Analysis." *Language* 28 (1952) 1-30. Reprinted in *The Structure of Language*, 355-83. Edited by Fodor and Katz.

_____. *Methods in Structural Linguistics*. Chicago: University of Chicago, 1951; Phoenix Books: *Structural Linguistics*, 1960.

Hockett, Charles. *A Manual of Phonology*. Baltimore: Waverly, 1955.

Hymes, Dell. Review of *Noam Chomsky*, by Justin Leiber. *Language* 48 (1972) 416-27. Reprinted in *On Noam Chomsky*, 316-32. Edited by Gilbert Harman.

Iwakura, Kunihiro. "The Syntax of Complement Sentences in English." *Linguistic Analysis* 3 (1977) 307-46.

Jackendoff, Ray. *Semantic Interpretation in Generative Grammar*. Cambridge: MIT, 1972.

Jacobs, Roderick A., and Rosenbaum, Peter S., eds. *Readings in English Transformational Grammar*. Waltham, MA: Ginn & Co., 1970.

Kasher, Asa. "Mood Implicatures: A Logical Way of Doing Generative Pragmatics." *Theoretical Linguistics* 1 (1974) 6-38.

Katz, Jerrold J. "Interpretive Semantics Vs. Generative Semantics." *Foundations of Language* 6 (1970) 220-59.

_____. *Semantic Theory*. New York: Harper and Row, 1972.

Kiparsky, Paul, and Kiparsky, Carol. "Fact." In *Progress in Linguistics*. Edited by Bierwisch and Heidolph. Reprinted in *Semantics*, 345-69. Edited by Steinberg and Jakobovits.

Lakoff, George. *Irregularity in Syntax*. New York: Holt, Rinehart & Winston, 1970.

Lakoff, Robin. Review of *Grammaire Générale de Raisonée*, edited by Herbert H. Brekle. *Language* 45 (1969) 343-64.

Lancelot, Claude, and Arnauld, Antoine. *General and Rational Grammar: The Port-Royal Grammar*. Edited and translated by Jacques Rieux and Bernard E. Rollin. The Hague: Mouton, 1975.
        First published in 1660; reprint edition, *Grammaire Générale et Raisonée*. Edited by Herbert H. Brekle. Stuttgart-Bad Canstatt: Friedrick Fromann, 1966.

Leech, Geoffrey. *Towards a Semantic Description of English*. London: Longmans, 1969.

Lees, Robert B. *The Grammar of English Nominalizations*. The Hague: Mouton, 1960.

Leiber, Justin. *Noam Chomsky: A Philosophical Overview*. Boston: G. K. Hall, 1975.

Lightfoot, David. "On Traces and Conditions on Rules." In
    Formal Syntax, 207-38. Edited by Culicover, Wasow and
    Akmajian.

Luce, Duncan; Bush, Robert B.; and Galenter, Eugene, eds. *Hand
    book of Mathematical Psychology* II. New York: Wiley, 196

Luce, Duncan; Bush, Robert B.; and Galenter, Eugene, eds. *Read
    ings in Mathematical Psychology* II. New York: Wiley, 195

Lyons, John. "Generative Syntax." In *New Horizons in Linguis-
    tics*, 115-39.

_____. *Introduction to Theoretical Linguistics*. Cambridge:
    Cambridge University, 1968.

_____. *Noam Chomsky*. New York: Viking, 1970.

_____, ed. *New Horizons in Linguistics*. Baltimore: Penguin
    1970.

Maclay, Howard. "Overview." In *Semantics*, 157-82. Edited by
    Steinberg and Jakobovits.

Moskowitz, Breyne. "The Acquisition of Language." *Scientific
    American* 239 (November, 1978) 92ff.

Nagel, Ernst; Suppes, Patrick; and Tarski, Alfred, eds. *Logic,
    Methodology and Philosophy of Science*. Stanford: Stanfor
    University, 1962.

Palmer, Frank R. *Grammar*. Baltimore: Penguin, 1971.

_____. "Why Auxiliaries Are Not Main Verbs." *Lingua* 47
    (1979) 1-25.

Quirk, Randolph; Greenbaum, Sidney; Leech, Geoffrey; and Svartv
    Jan. *A Grammar of Contemporary English*. New York: Semin
    Press, 1972.

Reibel, David A., and Schane, Sanford A., eds. *Modern Studies
    in English*. Englewood Cliffs, N. J.: Prentice-Hall, 1969

RenChao, Yuen. "Models in Linguistics and Models in General."
    In *Logic, Methodology and Philosophy of Science*, 558-66.
    Edited by Nagel, Suppes and Tarski.

Roberts, Paul. *English Sentences*. New York: Harcourt, Brace &
    World, 1962.

_____. *English Syntax: A Book of Programmed Lessons; An
    Introduction to Transformational Grammar*. New York:
    Harcourt, Brace & World, 1964.

_____. *Patterns of English*. New York: Harcourt, Brace, 195

_____. *Understanding English*. New York: Harper and Row, 19

_____. *Understanding Grammar*. New York: Harper and Row, 19

Rosenbaum, Peter S. *The Grammar of English Predicate Complement Constructions.* Cambridge: MIT, 1967.

Ross, John Robert. "A Proposed Rule of Tree-Pruning." In *Modern Studies in English*, 288-99. Edited by Reibel and Schane.

de Saussure, Ferdinand. *Cours de Linguistique Général.* Edited by Charles Bally and Albert Sechehaye. Paris: Payot, 1916. Translated by Wade Baskin: *Course in General Linguistics.* New York: McGraw-Hill, 1959.

Searle, John. "Chomsky's Revolution in Linguistics." In *On Noam Chomsky*, 2-33. Edited by Gilbert Harman.

Seiler, Hansjakob. "Abstract Structures for Moods in Greek." *Language* 47 (1971) 79-89.

Steinberg, Danny, and Jakobovits, Leon, eds. *Semantics: An Interdisciplinary Reader in Philosophy, Linguistics and Psychology.* Cambridge: Cambridge University, 1971.

Thorne, J. P. "Generative Grammar and Stylistic Analysis." In *New Horizons in Linguistics*, 185-97. Edited by John Lyons.

Turner, G. W. *Stylistics.* Baltimore: Penguin, 1973.

Wallis, John. *Grammar of the English Language.* Edited and translated by J. A. Kemp. New York: Longman, 1972. Originally published in 1660 as *Grammatica Linguae Anglicanae.*

Wasow, Thomas, and Roeper, Thomas. "On the Subject of Gerunds." *Foundations of Language* 8 (1972) 44-61.

INDEX OF NAMES

INDEX OF SUBJECTS

INDEX OF GREEK WORDS